DERREN BROWN
PORTRAITS

www.derrenbrownart.com

DERREN BROWN
PORTRAITS

Books

TRANSWORLD PUBLISHERS
61–63 Uxbridge Road, London W5 5SA
A Random House Group Company
www.rbooks.co.uk

First published in Great Britain in 2009 by Channel 4 Books
an imprint of Transworld Publishers

A CIP catalogue record for this book is available from the British Library.

ISBN 9781905026562

Addresses for Random House Group Ltd companies outside the UK
can be found at: www.randomhouse.co.uk
The Random House Group Ltd Reg. No. 954009

The Random House Group Limited supports The Forest Stewardship
Council (FSC), the leading international forest-certification organization.
All our titles that are printed on Greenpeace-approved FSC-certified paper
carry the FSC logo. Our paper procurement policy can be found at
www.rbooks.co.uk/environment

Design by Julia Lloyd
Image on p. 6 courtesy of Marc Hagan-Guirey
Printed and bound in Great Britain by Butler Tanner & Dennis Ltd, Frome, Somerset

2 4 6 8 10 9 7 5 3 1

Mixed Sources
Product group from well-managed
forests and other controlled sources
www.fsc.org Cert no. TT-COC-2139
© 1996 Forest Stewardship Council
FSC

opposite **OSCAR WILDE**

To my art teachers **Bob Brown**, **Derek Melotte**

and **Henry Maslin**

Having finished my maths exam early – more likely an indication of the number of questions left unanswered rather than any particular aptitude for the subject – I took from my remaining pile of untouched ruled Oxford A4s a single sheet and began to sketch Bob Chad. Mr Chad was our maths teacher and was supervising the exam that day, which may have been an O Level. I was in the last year to take such exams before those musty, black-gowned examinations of the old school gave way to shiny, young, sharp-suited, skinny-tied GCEs, and we all felt we were the last year not to have had our results fiddled with to make it look like we were getting cleverer.

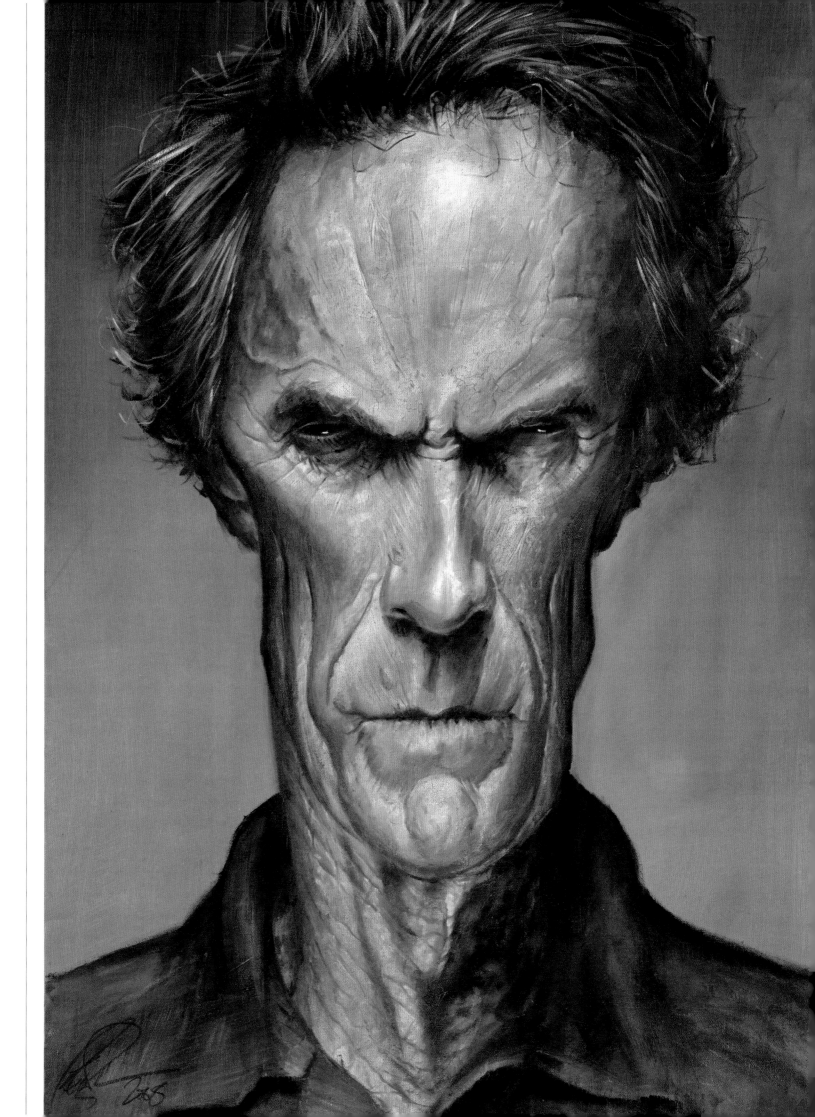

Mr Chad had – still has, I hope, though he was not a young

man at the time – the kind of extraordinary large ears known only

to teachers of a certain age and royalty of all ages. I vividly remember

the drawing I made that day, as I soon developed an obsession with

sketching this great and charming man: the ears, already described,

flapping flaccidly on either side of wide, raised cheekbones; a small

mouth with heavy lines on either end so that it resembled an H,

stretched out across the lower half of his face; a thin moustache;

a deep chin; enormous square glasses framing a series of converg-

ing wrinkles around tiny dots which formed the eyes. The picture

was not accurate, and neither were the many that followed. It was

recognizable and captured his gaunt, Nivenesque handsomeness,

but it missed many character points, which at that time I did not notice.

When I left school, Mr Chad asked for a sketch, and I happily gave one to him. I found out some years later from his daughter that he still had it. Perhaps framed in the toilet, which is a natural and happy home for these things. Wherever it was, I was very pleased.

Mr Chad was my first subject. After him came other teachers whose features lent themselves to exaggeration: Mr 'Basil' Smith (high forehead and a large, round nose with the end cleft to resemble a small bum); John 'Des' Clark (long upper lip, heavy eyelids and eyebrows); my own father, the swimming teacher (Del Boy meets Oliver Reed). I kept a folder, an old red ring-binder,

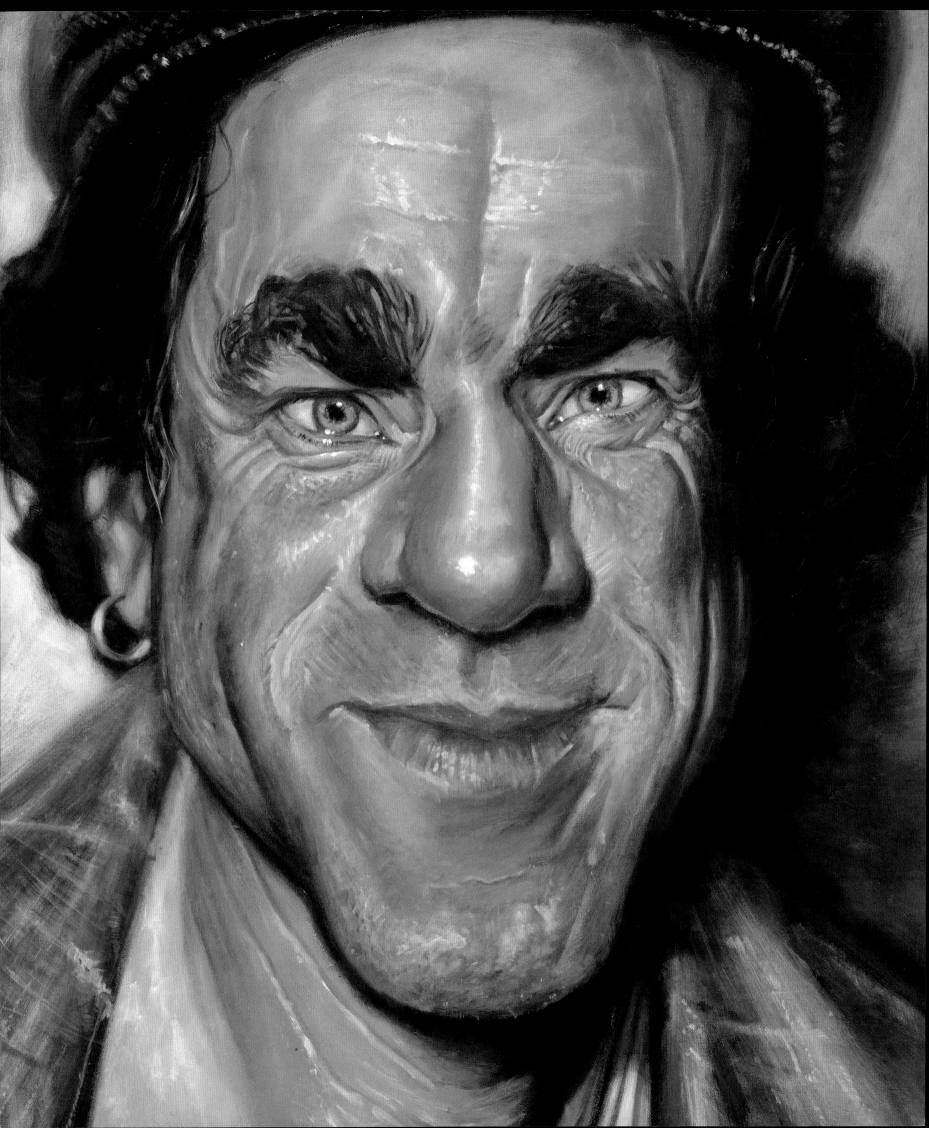

John Major

which slowly filled with pencil drawings of celebrities and teachers, the faces of the former largely copied from the pages of *Mad* magazine and then stuck on to diminutive bodies for further amusement value. Often they would wear tutus; sometimes I would write captions.

I enjoyed being a show-off and lapped up the notoriety the pictures brought me in the sixth-form. I was given my own notice board in the music school and every few days pictures of teachers were added or exchanged. New favourites emerged and occasionally I would catch staff laughing guiltily at their colleagues, hyperbolically rendered and cheekily displayed. Eventually it was removed: a few teachers were upset by some ruder illustrations and the notice board had to go.

Among these teachers an exemplary trio dominated my German language and literature career at school: Pattison, Clark and Polastro. Before and after my classes, and during breaks, I would leaf through imported copies of *Stern* magazine which featured, alongside some enjoyable soft porn, the caricatures of a German artist, Sebastian Kruger. Kruger's work (along with that of many other top caricaturists) is often copied, either by hand or by printer, taped up in front of street caricaturists' stalls around London and other tourist areas, and passed off as their own work.

If you've ever wondered why these pictures that advertise their skills appear pretty good but the drawing they're actually executing looks appalling, that's why. In almost all cases the images used to draw you in are by other artists – or, rather, 'actual' artists. Hats off to those street artists who are skilled enough to show their own work, and a pox upon those who insult us all with the utterly unethical and unjustifiable practice of passing off other people's work as their own.

Kruger's work focused mainly on German political characters I did not know, but his technique was superlative. These were not like the cheap cartoons or pedantic cross-hatched pen drawings I had seen before in British publications; they were solid, near-

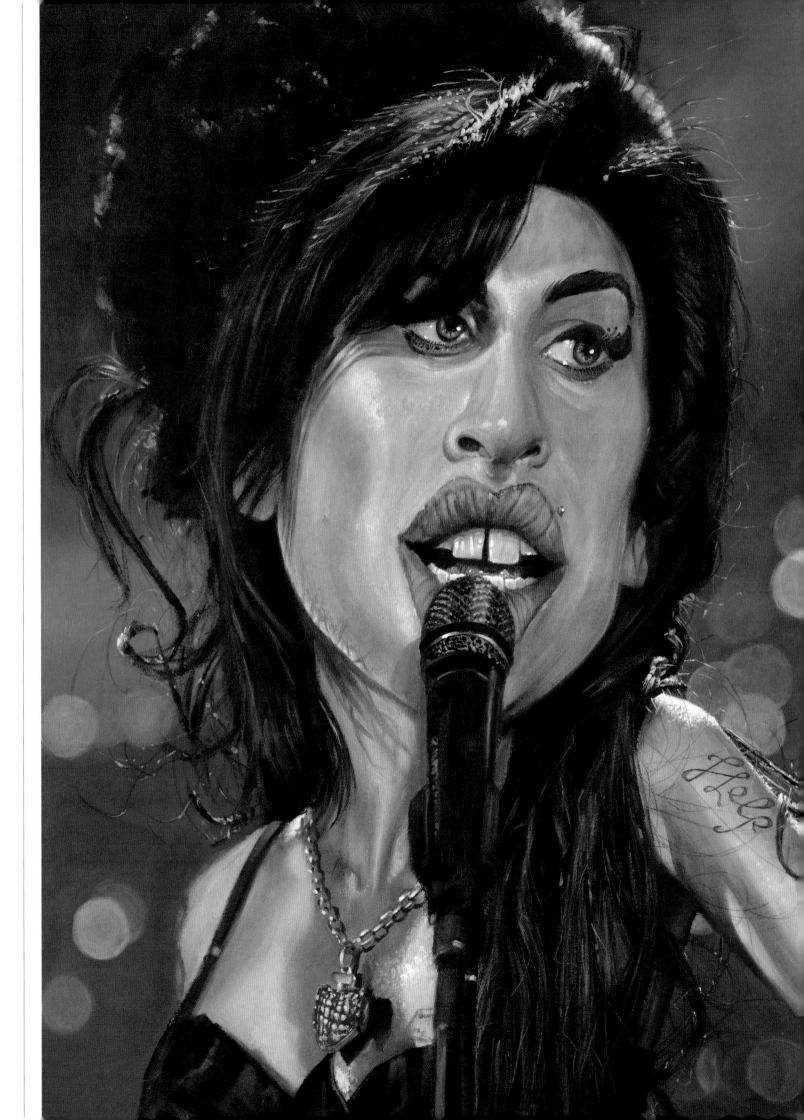

photo-realistic paintings that leapt from the page. I became hooked,

and when I visited Germany on school exchanges I searched out

more of his work. After A Levels, I spent my gap year near

Nuremberg in Bavaria, and while browsing one day in a bookshop

in a nearby town I found a collection of his work, *Alles Wird Gut!*

I spent a long time utterly absorbed in its pages, unable to believe

my luck, transported by the quality of its contents. I have a vague

feeling I may have stolen it; I can't remember for sure.

I have a vivid and curious memory from that day. As I was

walking across a marketplace I was passed by a heavy-set German

man coming in the opposite direction. I had the Kruger book under

my arm and I looked him right in the eye as he approached. I saw

'First he puts knitting needles in my arms, and now this.'

Robbie Williams

him in caricature. I saw his face as a three-dimensional, stretched and morphed exaggeration of itself. It was as clear as this nifty MacBook Air is before me now. At the same time I knew I was not just looking at a man with an unfortunate face. I was struck by the clarity of the hallucination, but I knew it was one. While I have never experienced that since, I am aware that I do not consciously exaggerate features. I just paint what I see.

At university my efforts were far more outrageous and owed much to a love of Gerald Scarfe and Ralph Steadman. I revelled in splattered paint or ink, and faces morphed into objects, following Scarfe's great images of Thatcher as a sweeping axe or grotesque pterodactyl. (Since discovering acrylic paints I have

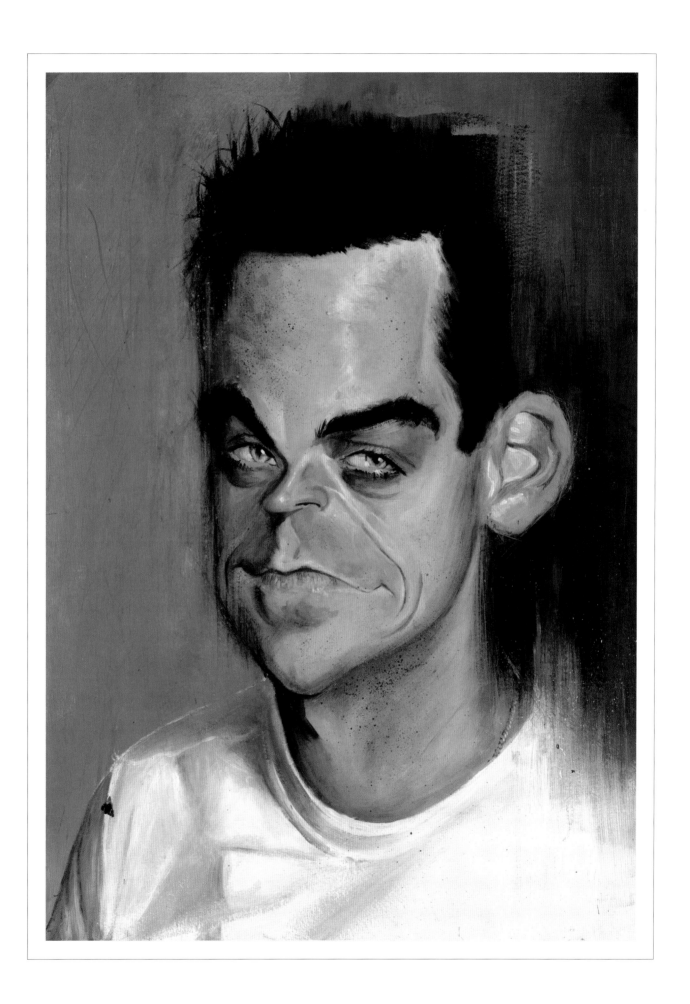

exaggerated the features of subjects less, and the result is something much softer.) But my love of Kruger's work remained. For me and many other 'serious' painters of caricature, it is an effort not to let his work become an obvious influence. For the painting of Bogart I used a photograph by Philippe Halsman as a source reference; fans of Kruger will recognize it as the German artist obviously used the same reference for his own, far superior, work. Since becoming aware of the resemblance, I have been more careful in my choice of source photograph.

After graduating from Bristol I lived in that beautiful city for another ten years and enjoyed an extraordinarily lazy and self-absorbed period which I miss enormously. I signed on and claimed

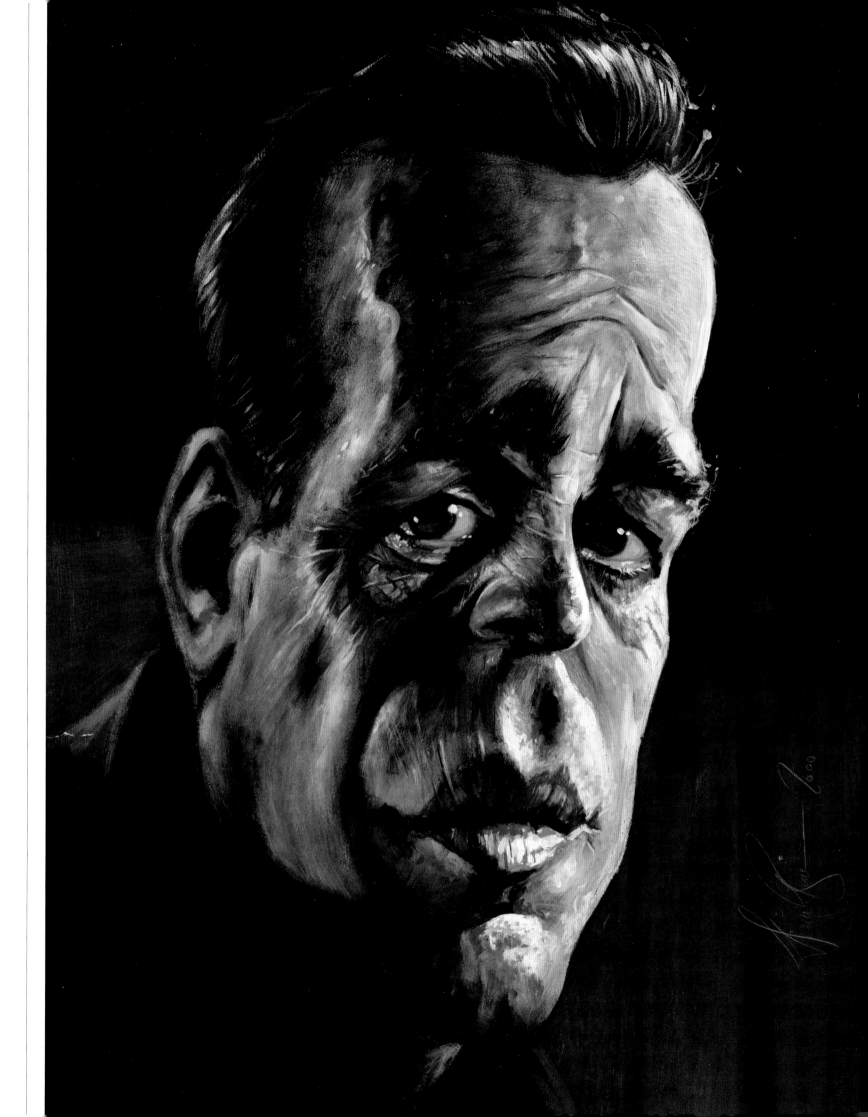

housing benefit until magic gigs provided enough to live on. Even when I was performing regularly I would most likely only be required a couple of nights a week so the rest of the time I ponced around town, read books, ate out on my own in gorgeous restaurants, and painted.

I frequently reflect that although I have become more 'successful' since and earn enough to enjoy the fancy goods and needless items upon which I now insist, I am probably no happier now than I was then. Pleasure and pain balance themselves out according to our dispositions, I think. In Bristol I had no respon- sibilities and all the time in the world to indulge myself in whatever whims took my fancy, but I would get lonely and bored from

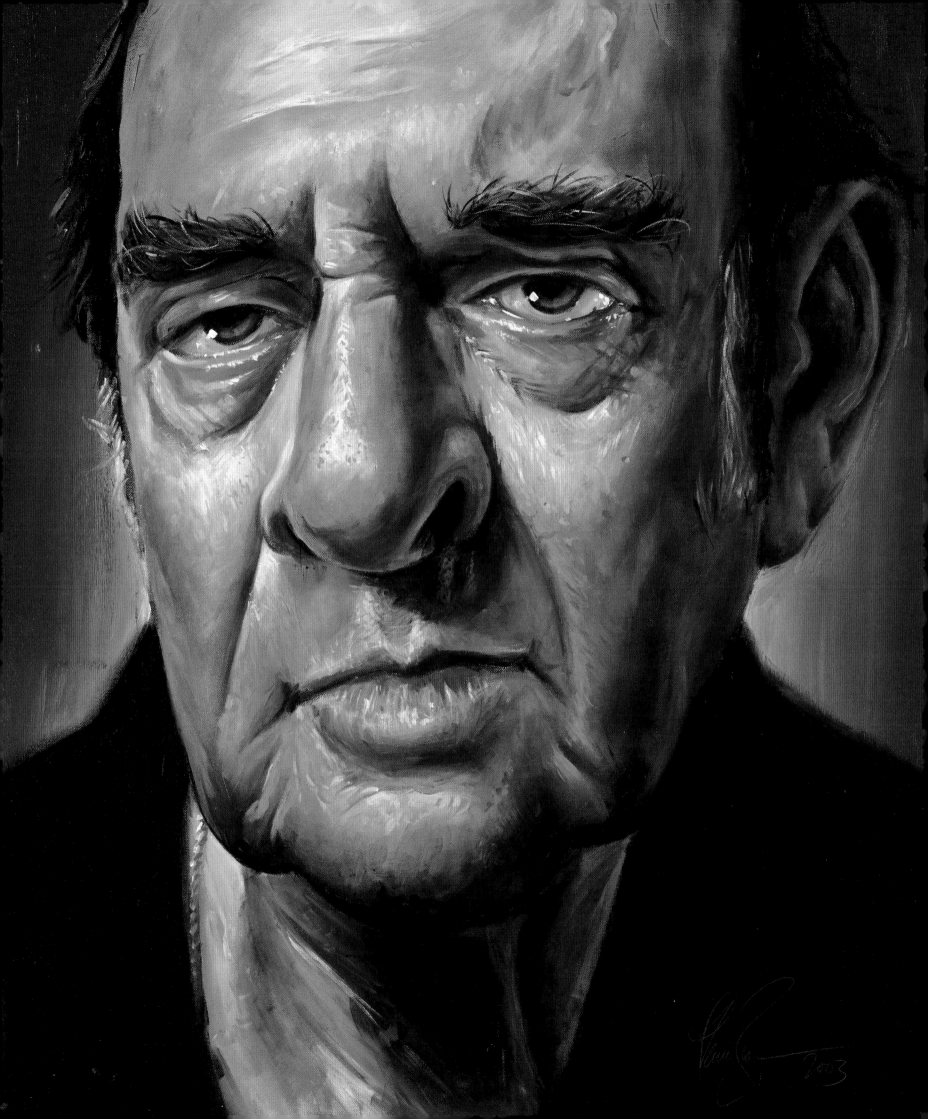

**'He's captured our original nature.
We're reptoids, you know.'**

Raymond Teller

time to time. Now I enjoy a lot of things I never considered would

be part of my life, but as the pleasure stakes have been raised, so

have the pains: loss of privacy, no spare time, dealing with stalkers

and crazies – the regular minor-celebrity whinges. The final

happiness level is no different than before.

I do miss the time to paint. The desire to focus exclusively on

painting now fluctuates in direct proportion to the level of

frustration with the TV and performance work. Most people in their

mid-thirties have started to question career decisions they made

in their twenties; this common fact provides part of the staple of

population stereotyping known to fraudulent psychics the world

over. I dream of packing in the day job, living in a big dirty studio

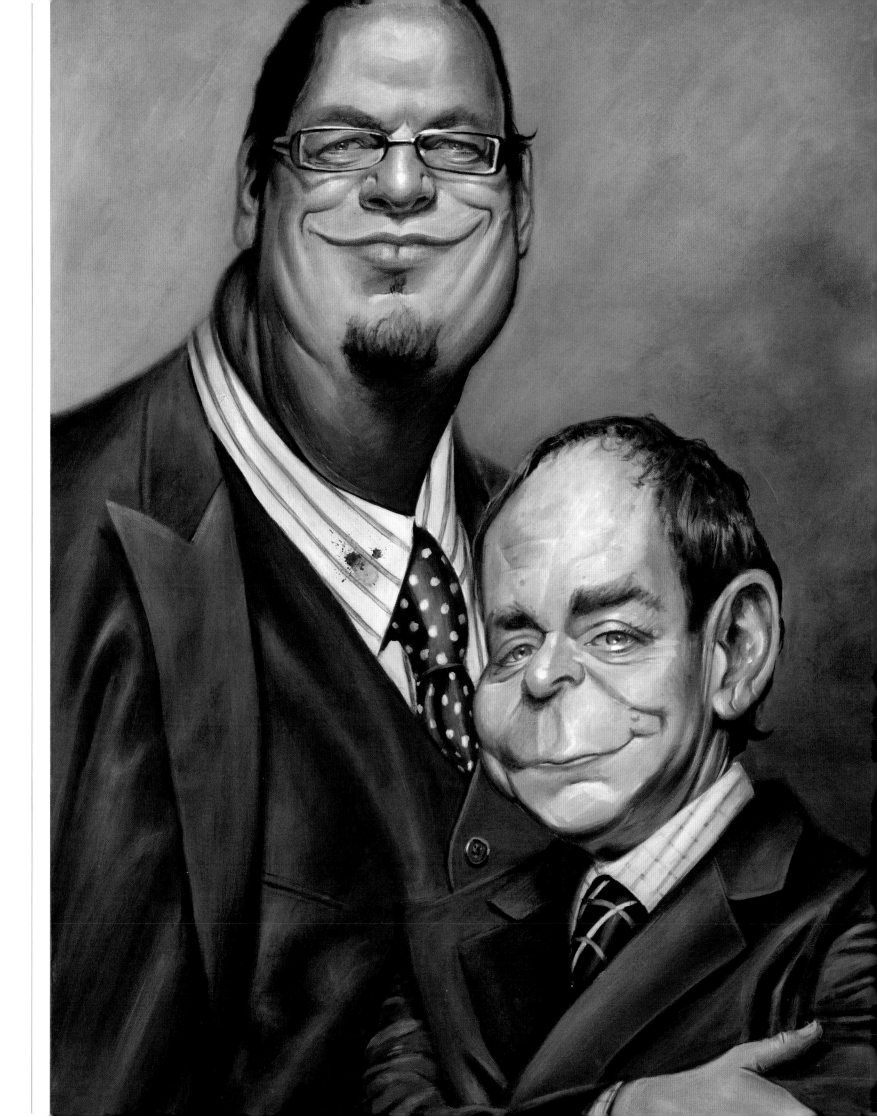

and painting people until I die (preferably of tuberculosis). But I'd miss my home cinema. So, for now, I just paint at weekends.

This book is a collection of those weekend paintings. Because I can't paint as often as I would like, the seventy or so pictures that fill these pages span several years, and vary noticeably in quality. Some I have gone back to and improved a little for this publication.

Perhaps through painting, I have a love of faces and the lines and shapes and bones that come together to form them. I can remember specifically the shape of a person's nose or eye or mouth long after meeting him. I used to draw only from memory; an ability to hold an image of a face as perfectly as possible was necessary in order to be able to do so. Now I am more interested in playing with realism than in just capturing essence, and as I said, I use photographic resources instead of pure memory. What I am very aware of, though, is my tendency to insist that people look like so-and-so when no one else can see the resemblance. This, I have realized over time, is due to finding specific resemblances between individual features which may not contribute much to the overall look of the face. A man might, for example, have the same mouth as Mozart, and to me the similarity will be striking, but no amount of explanation will convince others, who are more likely to judge similarity by a person's eyes or the general shape of his face.

I imagine an impressionist might find similarities between some aspect of the timbre or placing of one voice and another, which would be equally pointless trying to explain in mixed company. Indeed, I have always had a love for vocal impressions, and think there is a clear parallel between the arts of impersonation and caricature. The impersonator must presumably develop a talent for hearing voices a little more clearly, along with an ability to dissect and place aspects of a voice to which the rest of us would find it hard to pay such focused attention. He must then be able to reproduce what he has analysed. Equally, he can then exaggerate or accurately reproduce as he wishes.

One particular comment I sometimes hear in response to my pictures is that I have 'captured' so-and-so through a particular

opposite **MARLON BRANDO**

expression. This I find interesting, as although I am of course

attempting to capture a detailed likeness, I wonder why a

particular expression might seem somehow to manifest this

essence more than some other. I might understand it more if I heard

this comment only when I had painted the subject exhibiting

a facial expression one would expect anyone immediately to

associate with him or her (Jack Nicholson's devilish grin, for

example, or a perpetually happy friend's infectious smile), but this

is not the case. There seems to be something inherent in the surface

arrangement of a person's features that we connect with a very clear

sense of personality. People we know with clear traits – optimism,

arrogance, aggression – seem to have them permanently etched

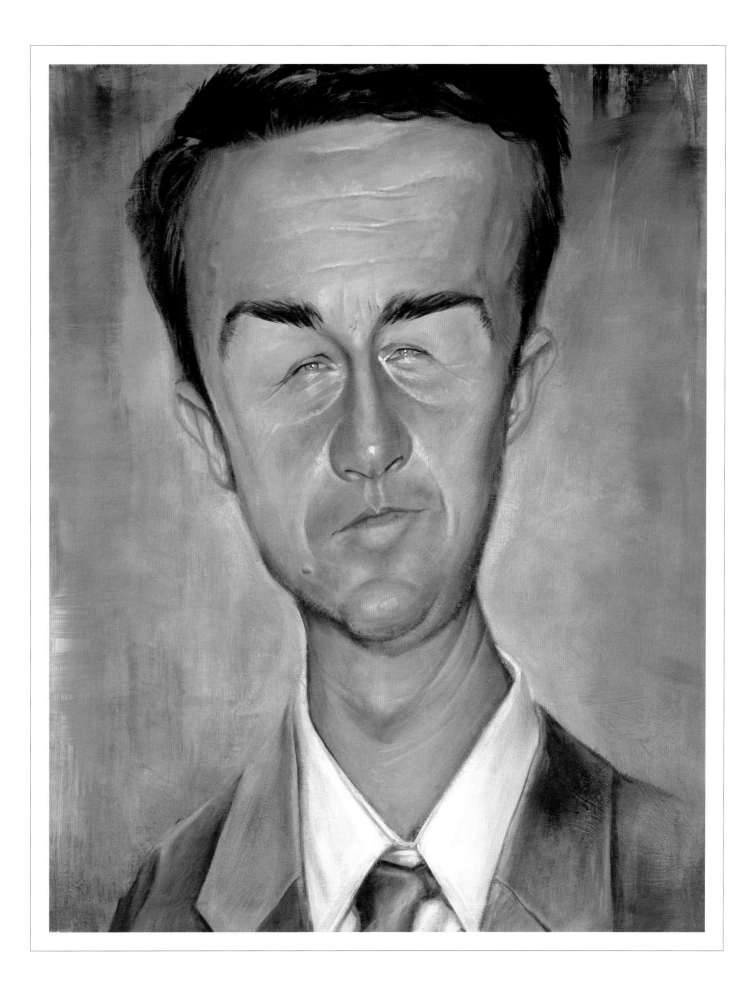

Brad Pitt

in the placing of their eyes, nose and mouth, the formation of their eyebrows and the thrust and shape of their face. And when we think upon a friend's or enemy's face, the feelings that image automatically engenders seem to support the idea that something is inherent in that picture to make us feel that way.

Of course the relationship between features and personality is much more fickle but we act as if it were straightforward. We can look at a photograph of another person and have absolutely no sense of their character, but we're very good at making it up. Several sociological experiments have been undertaken where a

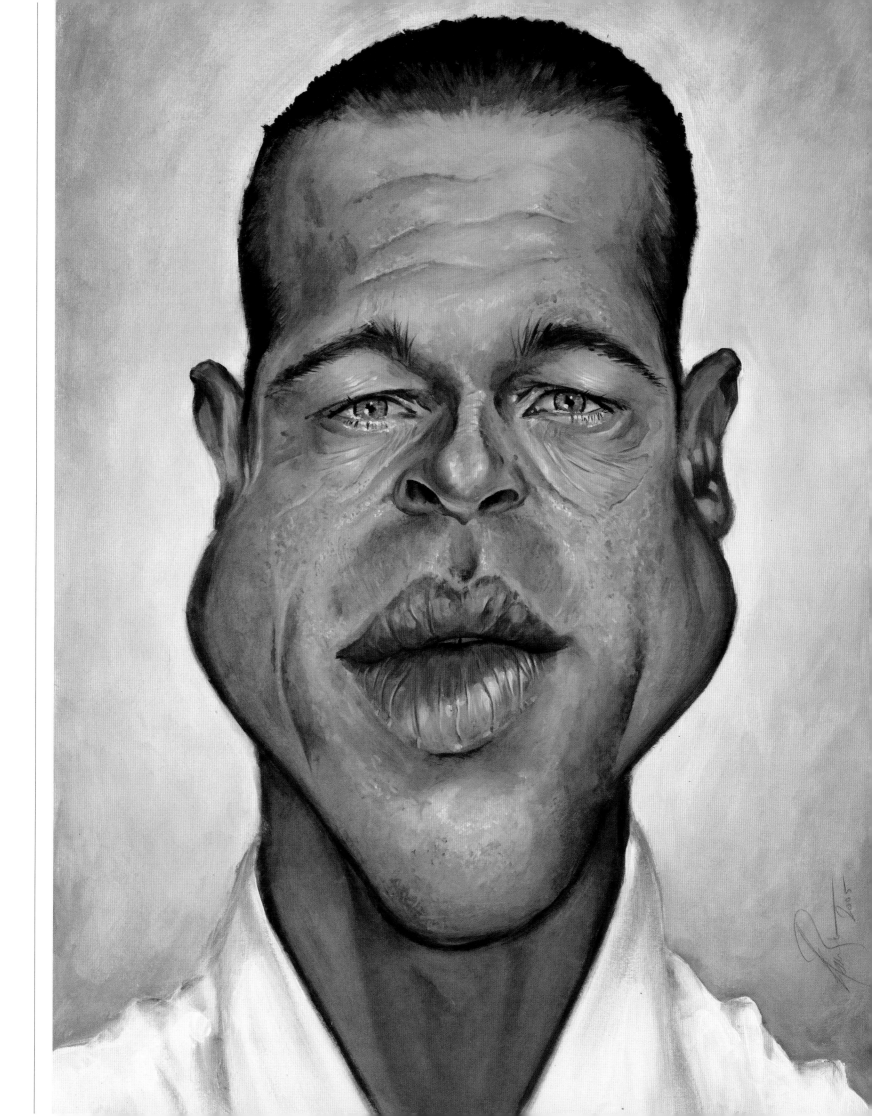

mock jury is told tales of fictional crimes and given photographs of the supposed defendant. Some juries are given images of people who do not conform to the facial stereotype of a criminal (fresh-faced, blond hair, large, clear eyes) and others are shown photographs of bearded characters and men with close-set eyes and the like which fit in more with the classic image of a 'villain' we have absorbed, presumably, since the days of early photography and silent movies. Routinely, juries showed a bias towards finding the bearded, thicker-set type of face to be that of a guilty man.

In another experiment, where subjects heard details of two crimes – one tale of negligence and another of fraud – juries even tended to decide that a defendant with a higher forehead and

opposite CHRISTOPHER WALKEN

chubbier cheeks (therefore more 'baby-faced') was the one guilty

of negligence whereas one with deeper, thicker features must be

the fraudster.

I do not know whether the members of the 'juries' in these

experiments were then questioned about their recently

demonstrated biases, but presuming that none of them would admit

to being prejudiced against men with beards and dark eyes and

the like, the results raise the obvious question of how fairly a black

defendant can expect to be viewed before a white jury. (Malcolm

Gladwell's enjoyable book *Blink!* contains some very interesting

experiments for the reader to try, which suggest an unavoidable

racist bias in more of us than we'd care to admit.)

opposite **CAMERON DIAZ**

'As with the best portraits, I was at first
shocked by Derren's view of me: surely my
ski-slope nose is not quite so prominent? And
are my lips actually made of rubber? But then
I looked again and I acknowledged that though
viewed through a fish-eye lens, this was me:
my eyes exactly, the sharply raised eyebrow,
the deep bags. And that great flapping ear.
And then I decided that I liked the sensuous
pugnacity, the challenge and the questioning
gaze. I have a copy of it myself and consult
it from time to time if I'm feeling timid.'

Simon Callow

opposite **SIMON CALLOW**

So, we are happy to read what we like into features, and that interpretation need bear no relation to the person's actual personality. On occasion I have painted a caricature as a commission of a person I do not know, and the finished article has been greeted with the same response of delight at how I have captured a real personality. Yet I have no sense of the subject's character. Any sense that might 'come through' somehow in the picture is nothing that can be attributed to intention on my part.

Anyway, do our characters not change enormously given the situation we are in? A happy and gracious disposition might give way to a terrible temper in some circumstances. An outgoing personality might be balanced with times of real introversion.

Working psychics need only touch upon contrasting traits such as these to have the client feel that she is being deeply and accurately understood as the complex person she is. So who are we to decide that the aspect of a person's character we see matches the perceptions of other people? And how can a caricature capture a recognizable essence of a person if we are fluctuating, complex entities full of exhausting contradictions?

I remember very vividly sitting in stands with my mother watching my father, who has always been a fine and respected swimming trainer, supervise a race. I was possibly six years old. To my left sat a lady with the sternest expression I had ever seen. She looked really *mean*. And when I say that, you will see aspects of

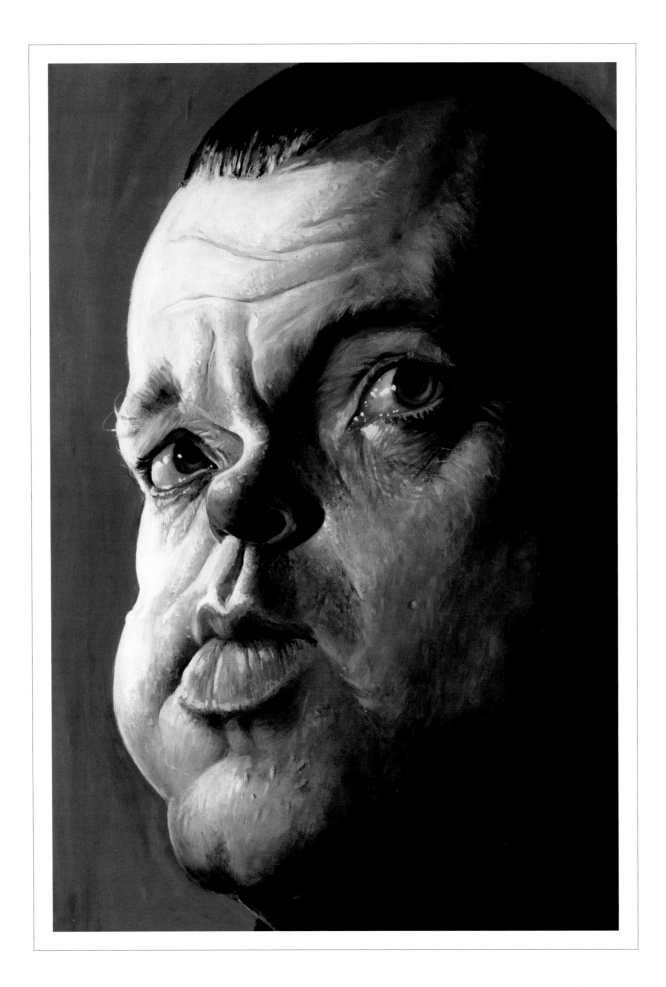

her expression clearly: eyebrows that point downwards towards the nose; tight, small mouth; beady eyes; a fierce glare. Mean. I was quite frightened by her, although she had not said a word. I imagine that I kept staring at her, watching her react to the races she was watching. At some point I needed to talk to her; I think I dropped something which had rolled under her legs and I needed to ask her to shift a little so I could reach it. I found the courage to make this request, and when she spoke to me she was the sweetest lady imaginable. I was so shocked. I talked to my mother about it later, at some length. This was the first time I heard the expression 'don't judge a book by its cover', as my mother explained to me that a mean-looking person might not actually *be* mean.

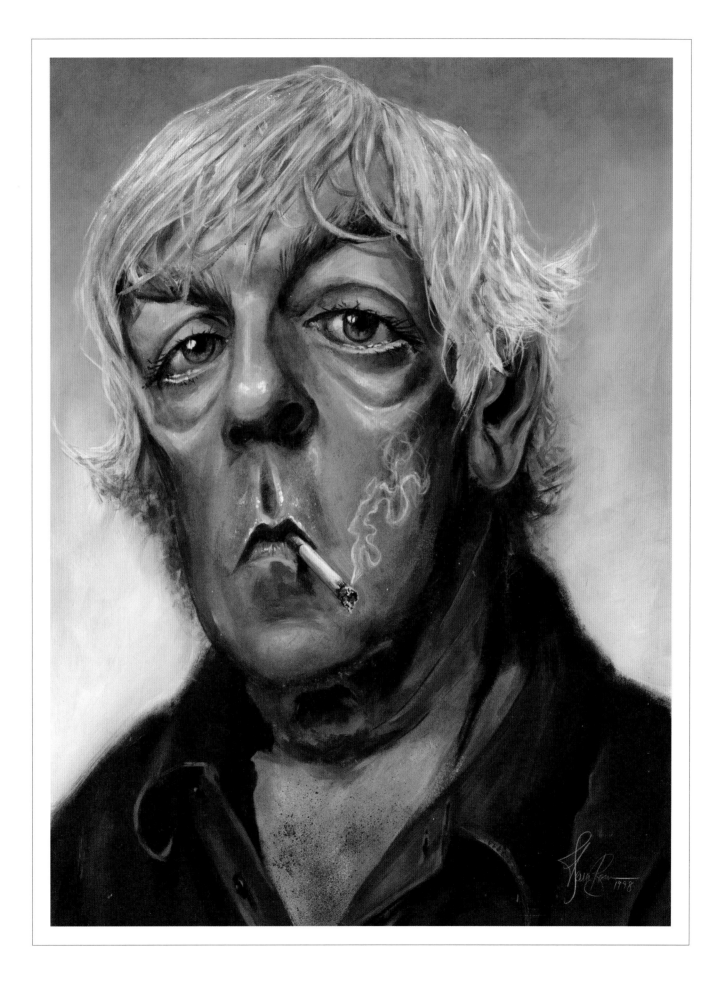

Since then, and the more I heard people talk about capturing

a personality in the features, I have pondered the question of how

features and personality connect. Was the woman at that

swimming match an exception? If so, why does an open, friendly

person so often seem to show that in his face? Why does an

aggressive type so often flag up his temper in his pinched

physiognomy? Or is there no link, and I am merely noticing patterns

where I can find them? Are there just as many aggressive people

with the most flaccid of faces?

It's not too far removed from the question of why rich people

tend to be more attractive. Rich people, we imagine, move in a

world where appearance means more, where grand social

occasions are frequent, and it is to their advantage to fit in by looking

the best they can, in the same way we all like to chime with the

look and sound of our peers. Also, rich people have easier access

to the sort of clothes and products that will make the best of what

they have. Undoubtedly there is also a pride that comes more

frequently with social advantage than disadvantage, and pride is

often manifested in wanting to look good.

Viewed from the other angle – why do attractive people do

better in life? – it is easy to see the social advantages of being

physically attractive that might lead to such an individual being

favoured over less good-looking peers as he moves through his career

and life. We like to form relations with attractive people, and when

we see people who look good, we tend to show them our best and most generous side. In the same way that many celebrities might go through their life receiving 'special treatment', attractive people are not far behind. If the result for those people is a life full of meeting pleasant people who want to know them, understandably their own disposition is likely to be more confident. So not only do richness and attractiveness often go hand in hand, so too do attractiveness and confidence. And confidence is far more likely to lead to financial success than shyness.

So, for those of us whose looks do not automatically trigger simple magnetic attraction, can we talk about a real link between character and face? If friendly people look friendly, why is that?

And if aggressive people carry their temper in their faces, how does that happen? This begs two other questions. Firstly, does the face cause the personality rather than vice versa? Secondly, why do we respond so instinctively to the mapping of features? These features, caused by the shape of bone and muscle tissue – should they really play such a role in how we deal with people?

The lady at the swimming match might actually have been quite an aggressive woman for all I know. Perhaps a polite if precocious kid with platinum-blond curly locks asking her if she'd be kind enough to move her feet bypassed her normal sternness and caused a temporary melting of her usual icy temperament that would have astonished her few friends. What was clear to me at

opposite **GEORGE BUSH**

that age was that as she looked stern, she would be treated *as if* she were stern by people who spoke to her.

Could that be enough to *make* someone stern? If one is treated as a fool, one becomes happier to act like one. In another sociological experiment, teachers were given what they thought were projected academic results for their new class. In fact these predictions were random and bore no relation to how clever the children were. The result was that the kids the teachers *believed* were the cleverer ones ended up achieving the better results. Treating the children as more gifted actually made them do better. And the kids believed to be less bright fared the worst.

Time and time again the importance of encouragement has

been demonstrated in schools and at work. Many of us will, I'm sure, have memories of a teacher who was new to us at the start of an academic year reviving our interest in a subject by giving us good results and treating us as someone with an aptitude for that subject. I spent my entire secondary school career hating maths and thinking I couldn't do it, purely because I was told I wasn't much good at it in *primary* school. I would love to hear a teacher telling a new class of problem kids that she had heard bad stories about them but didn't believe them to be true; in fact, she believed them to be the best class in the school. Equally, if a child is naughty and is routinely told that he is bad, this can have a damaging effect that does not arise if the child believes he is a *good* boy who has for some reason *behaved* badly. Framing bad behaviour as just that, *behaviour* rather than *identity*, can make a huge difference in making useful shifts with children.

Perhaps disappointingly for the caricaturist, research seems to point to the conclusion that we are no good at all at telling what people are like merely from looking at their faces. The reality is that we probably have to let go of the idea that character really does reliably show through in the features. If it did, we'd be better at judging people simply by looking at them. However, while we are poor at drawing accurate conclusions about character from faces, we tend to draw reliably *similar* (and usually mistaken) conclusions. In other words, we are quick to jump to the same

judgements as other people about what certain faces say about

a person. Despite that consensus, we'd still all probably be wrong.

I think the apparent coincidence of a generally grumpy face and

a grumpy person is more likely to be due to other factors, for

example a person's clothes and general appearance, which will

tell you a lot about the individual and will push you towards

drawing certain conclusions about how that person is likely to

act. We focus on the face and easily attribute our judgements to

its expression and interplay of features, but the reality is that if

the same face were transposed on to a very different body and

dressed and groomed differently, the chances are we would 'read'

it very differently.

A second reason why we might incorrectly believe we can judge

a person by her face comes from our tendency to look for evidence

that confirms our preconceptions and to ignore evidence to the

contrary. In many tests, people have shown that if they are given

information about the character of an individual ahead of

meeting him, and are then told to ask him questions to see whether

the character assessment was true, they repeatedly ask questions

designed to *confirm* the assessment, and therefore are very likely

to decide that it was an accurate one. For example, if we are told

that so-and-so is an extrovert and want to see if it is true, we will

tend to ask if he likes to go out to parties and so on; we don't as

often think to ask questions about how frequently he likes to spend

above & opposite **JOHN GIELGUD**

time alone. We therefore end up with a conclusion that is biased towards what we were told was true in the first place.

You may have been in a situation where person X unfairly told you negative things about person Y before you met the latter for the first time. You became friends with Y, but found it took a long while to get over the preconceptions with which X had filled your head. This is most likely due to the fact that you could not help but look for examples of Y's behaviour that confirmed the negative reports you had been given. Evidence to the contrary somehow gets circumscribed or is seen as less than typical of Y's real personality.

I imagine we do the same when we meet people whose faces

opposite **BILLY JOEL**

suggest a particular character trait. Those faces most of us (erroneously) decide are friendly, aggressive, intelligent or whatever predispose us to look for behaviour that confirms our suspicions. When we start talking to the person, we are likely to take on the role appropriate to our predisposition: if we decide that person looks very open and friendly, we are likely to relax and be ourselves, whereas an aggressive or stern-looking face might prompt us to tread more carefully. Unless the individual we are dealing with surprises us by acting very differently from how we expected, our behaviour is likely to exacerbate things and confirm our conviction that he is indeed how we imagined. For the more we adopt a certain role with a person, the more likely he is to take the corresponding role

for himself in dealing with us. If we are relaxed and friendly with people because they appear to be friendly themselves, they are more likely to act in a pleasant and relaxed way. Those people may decide the world is a friendlier place as a consequence, while the next man whose face happens to conform more to a 'stern' stereotype spends his time being approached with trepidation.

So the fact that we rarely just look at a face in isolation when judging character, and our tendency to look for traits that confirm what we are expecting, suggest to me that we shouldn't talk about the caricaturist capturing a personality in his faces. What he certainly does is create a picture more unmistakably *of that person* than a simple photograph.

Since technology has allowed us to morph and combine multiple images to form composites, social psychologists interested in face perception have been combining faces of large numbers of people to see what an 'average' face might look like, and how we might respond to it. Interestingly, there is a tendency for us to find these composite faces more attractive. Even when a normal 'straight' line drawing of a face has been 'uncaricatured' by computer, we tend to rate the result as more attractive. By 'uncaricatured', I mean that the drawn face is measured and compared to an average face, and then rather than the differences being *exaggerated* (as with a caricature) they are *lessened*. These composite uncaricatured images have a certain blandness about them, but we do tend to rate them as attractive. By exaggerating features, a caricaturist takes the face further and further away from this average, and in doing so should make the face increasingly recognizable and, it follows, less attractive.

We recognize one another in a number of ways: first by specific features (we remember a person's goatee, for example), then by the relationships between features (we learn that the eyes are close together or far apart), and finally in a kind of 'holistic' way (where we recognize a friend we are familiar with but not with reference to any specific aspect of her face). Caricaturists exaggerate these features and relationships between features and arrive at something that should still work as a whole. The result is that every measurable

aspect of that face which distinguishes it from a baseline has been multiplied, and the resulting image, we can say, is *more* like that person than that person is. Or should be, if the picture is successful.

Perhaps this is why it's harder to paint famous actresses. Looked at with an eye for the extreme, the standards of female beauty involve a regression to a younger, more symmetrical, 'simpler' face. Cosmetics are used to cover any blemishes and help soften any prominent features that distract from an almost doll-like ideal. Plenty of strong-featured women are every bit as beautiful as those who conform more to this ideal, but they tend to be described with epithets such as 'unconventionally' attractive, which betrays our tendency to embrace a particular dull, conventional attractiveness first and

foremost. Looking at images of Hollywood actresses in magazines, I am often struck by the tendency of photographers and those who work in image post-production to remove as many shadows as possible from female faces, thus doing their best to lose the character of the nose (a larger nose is a signifier of the male face, so much is done to downplay the nose in order to boost femininity in these pictures), jaw-line and the areas around the eyes. The result is that famous, attractive women who might otherwise make good subjects for caricature prove troublesome, for they somehow look less like themselves as their features are exaggerated and overplayed. (Those readers who remember *Spitting Image* well enough might now understand why the Diana puppet never quite looked

right, if the remarkable Fluck and Law don't mind me saying.)

As with 'conventionally attractive' women, so also with children, and for the same reason. Male (adult) beauty, however, which more happily embraces strong, craggy features and hard lines (photographers are far more likely here to use strong shadows to enhance men's features rather than over-expose or employ the airbrush to lose them), undeniably lends itself better to the caricaturing process. For this reason there are far more men in this collection than women. The women that do appear tend to be older (as their features have become more defined).

For those interested in the processes I follow to choose my subjects and then paint them, I shall explain.

'This is much more than a caricature. Derren has captured my intensity and distilled it into the depths of my eyes. When I look at this painting I can feel the colour tones of the skin change, as if blood is pulsing just beneath the surface. The expression seems to change too, but I cannot define the subtle differences each time I look at it, because all of my attention is captured by the eyes. It is a sensation completely unlike looking into a mirror – instead of seeing my reflection, I feel as though I'm seeing myself.

I have been a painter and an artist throughout my career – my designs are not limited to canvas but have been reproduced as pottery, jewellery and even watches. In the early seventies I studied with Salvador Dali, a genius who knew without doubt that his gift was literally divine: it came from God, and he wielded it with supernatural energy. Dali taught me that art without belief is mere imitation – and art with belief was the greatest force on earth. It truly is Creation.

Derren's powers as an artist and a mentalist fascinate me. Whether he is holding a paintbrush or a microphone, he acts without limitations. Anything is possible to him. His self-belief is total, and consequently we believe in him too. He can convince anyone of anything, and that is because he has learned the power of convincing himself. I predict his career will take more fascinating twists in the near future, and that he will carry off impossible feats with aplomb and conviction.'

Uri Geller

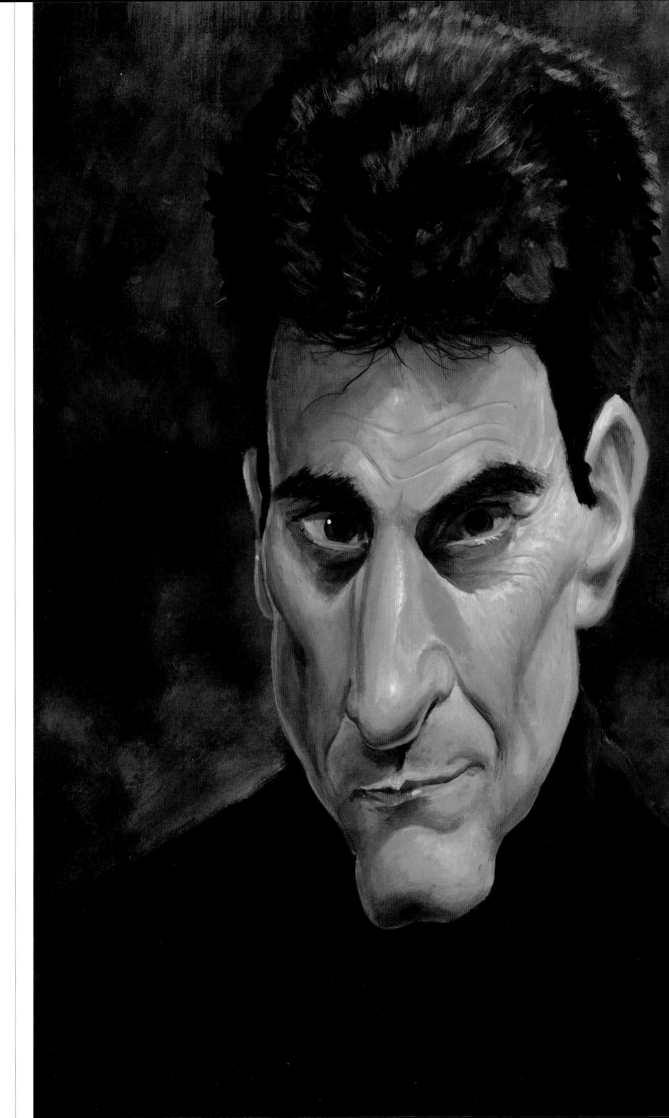

above & opposite **ANTHONY HOPKINS**

Anthony Hopkins

I find certain subjects returning again and again to my thoughts. When he or she has strong, varied 'images' an obsession can develop to try to capture a subject in different ways. There is, for example, Anthony Hopkins: the man with the intensity of Lecter and other monsters, but also, by contrast, the unassuming, now-at-peace-with-himself character we see in television interviews. Both are deeply appealing, and enjoyable to try to portray. (The brooding, difficult, younger Hopkins would be a different painting altogether, an enjoyable project for the future.)

The younger Woody Allen gives us the clownish incarnation

Woody Allen

with the wafting ginger hair and the upwardly cast eyes that signify self-appointed low status, desire for approval, and the visionary look of the dreamer. But as an older man and icon of brilliance he looks downwards, on a world of feeling and internal conflict; his drooping expression is no longer clownish but introverted, an image of retreat and baffled shyness atop his academic green pullovers and corduroy slacks.

Jack Nicholson, by contrast, seems shaped and engineered by star-makers to give us a clear sense of what he is and represents, and the images we have of him across his career largely inhabit

above & opposite **WOODY ALLEN**

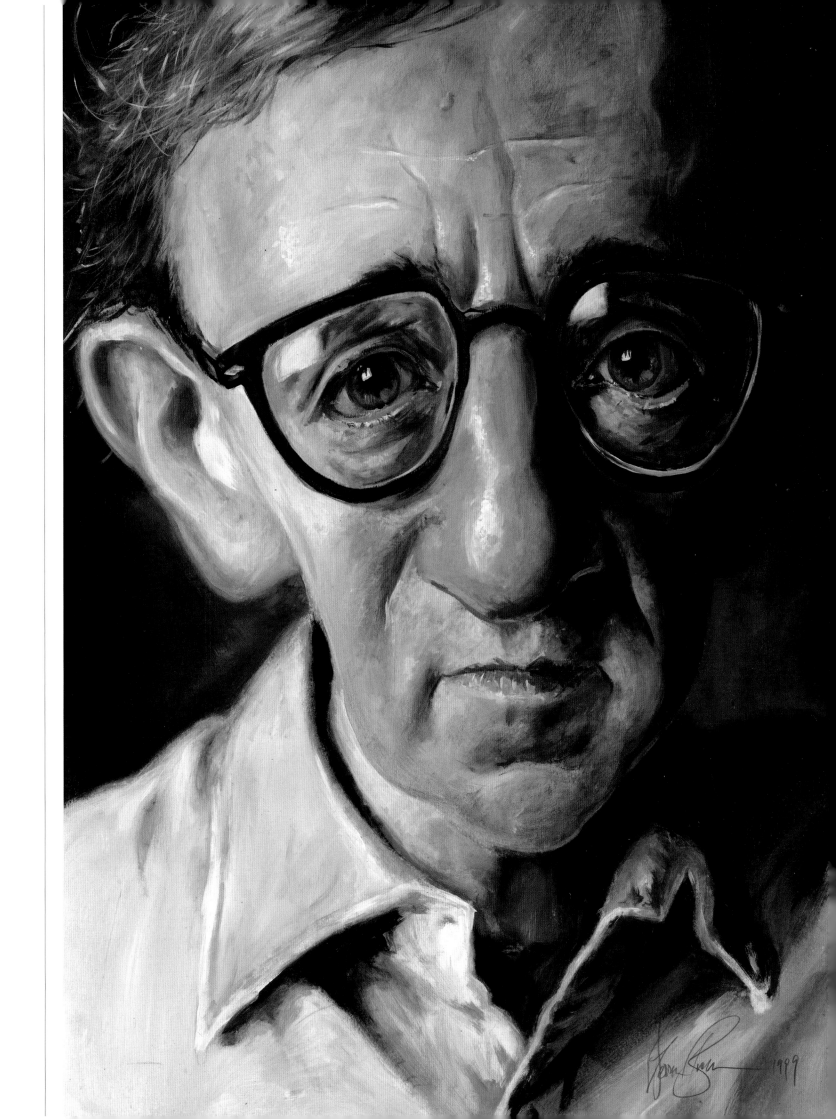

the same world. He remains the iconic playboy, regardless of reality,

and in that sense we delight in the older Jack because he seems to

be a young spirit caught in the body of an unapologetic, unabashed

older man. Interestingly for me, we think of him as 'devilish': that

epithet follows him around everywhere, and fits the image of him

grinning behind a huge cigar in luxury surroundings; but it would

seem that it really only comes from his famous eyebrows, which

happen to dip and reach and sprout a little before diving down towards

the top of his nose. Such a brow arrangement, when combined with

a grin and a downwards tilt of the head, gives us the classic 'devil'

pose we recognize, a blend of evil (angry eyebrows tell us to keep

away) and a come-hither sparkle and smile. Hence the idea of evil

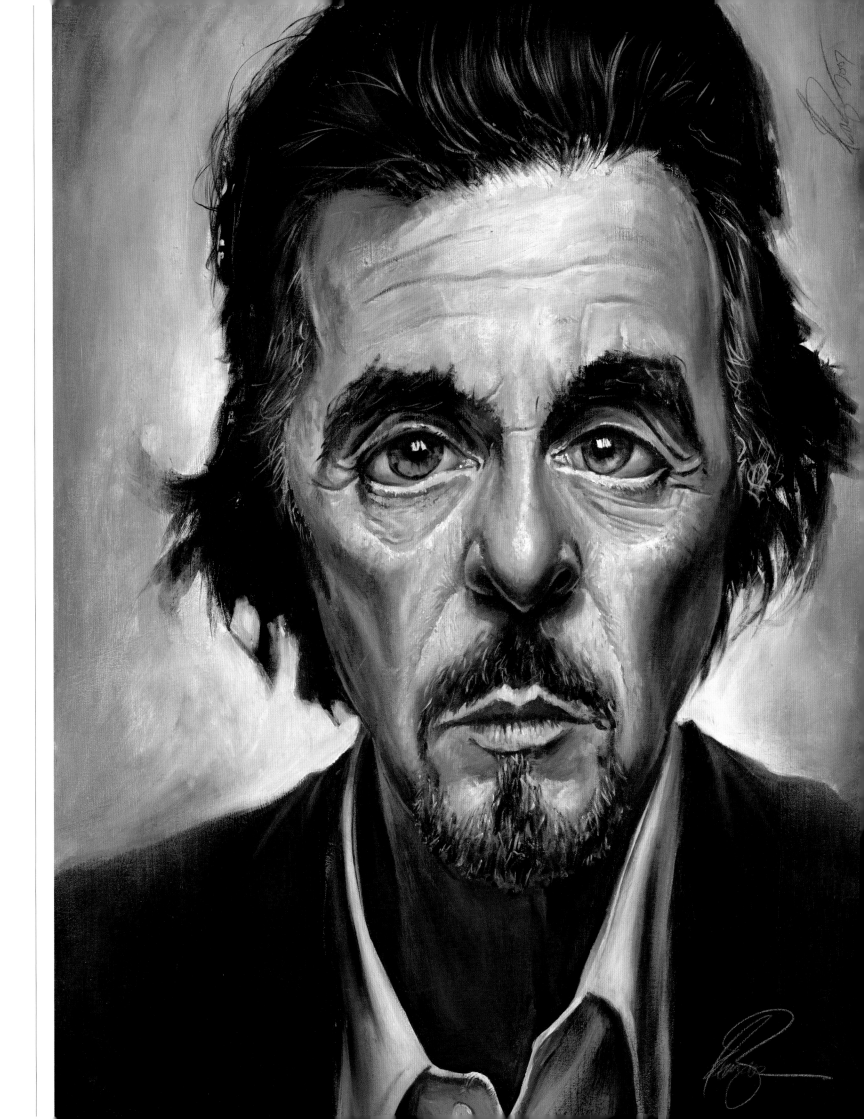

'Me after my last stunt.'

David Blaine

temptation, the feeling of 'you want to, though you know you

shouldn't' we associate with wickedness. It's a purposeful conflict

of opposing messages being given, not incomparable to a coy,

seductive look that says 'no, I'm shy' (by half-turning away and feigning

disinterest) while at the same time promising an intimate 'yes' (by

holding eye contact and parting the lips to hint at a kiss).

Nicholson has made this devilish expression his trademark,

and impressionists use that look to help audiences identify him.

Christian Slater has modelled himself on the older actor,

frequently striking the same pose – particularly when he took on

Nicholson's famous role in the stage version of *One Flew Over the*

Cuckoo's Nest – and training his eyebrows to resemble those of the

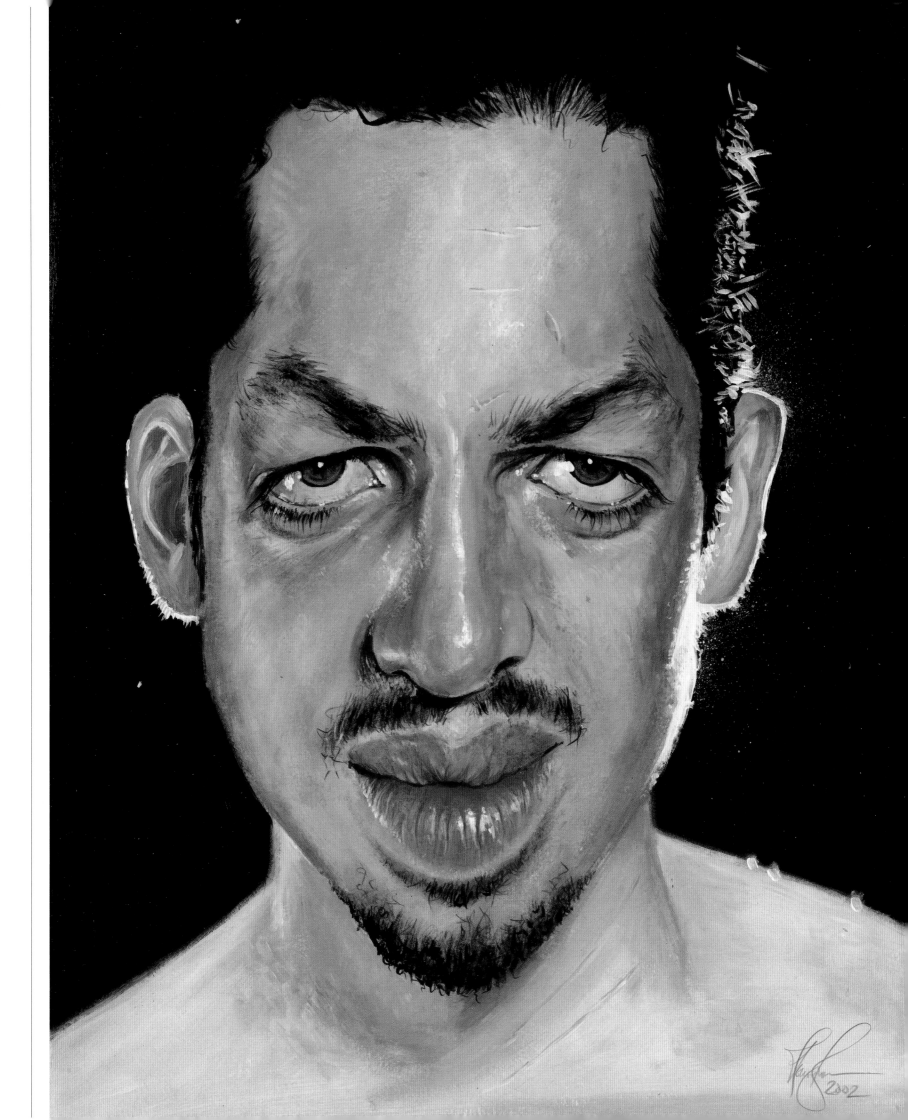

above & opposite **JACK NICHOLSON**

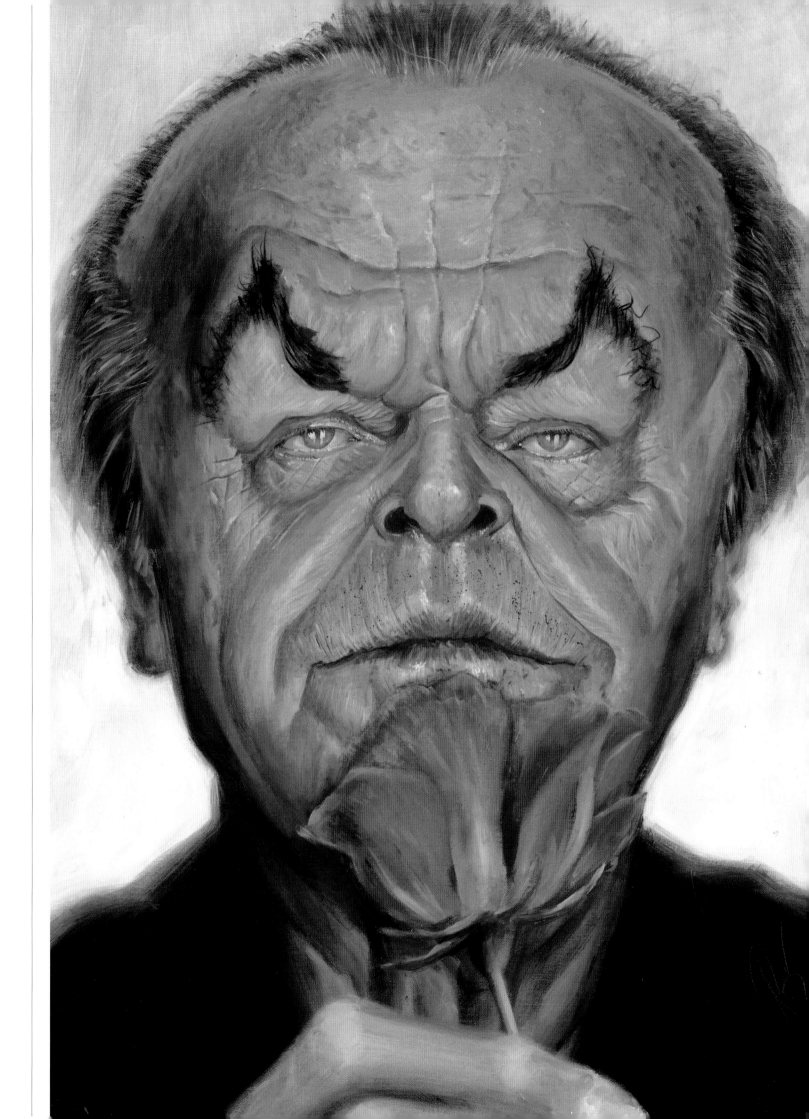

man one may take to be his idol. Nicholson appears to us to be authentically 'devilish' through and through, not just in looks but also in character. An iconography has been sustained through a chance arrangement of eyebrows. If Jack had Woody's plaintive eyebrows, we would never think of him in that way.

The choice of subject is occasionally driven by finding a great photographic source, but more often by developing an interest in that person and loving the idea of committing him or her to canvas. Rufus Wainwright was one of these: I discovered his music through a mutual friend and listened to his albums non-stop while painting.

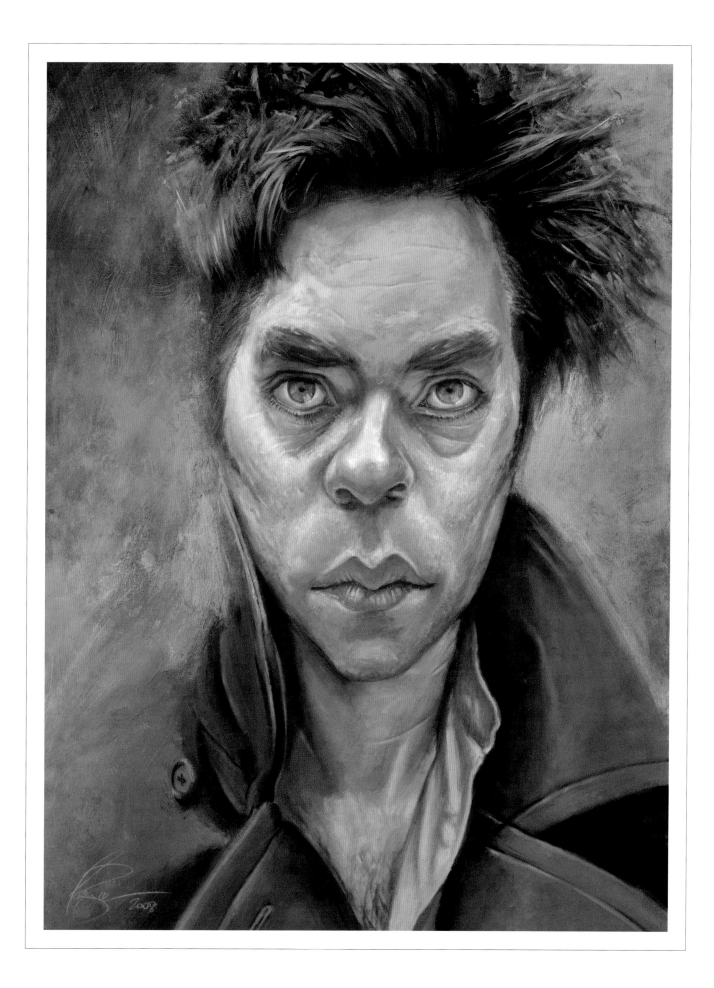

His face did not scream out to be caricatured, unlike some others,

and not being a television watcher or knowledgeable about modern

music I was not familiar with his face. But as an enthusiastic admirer

I very much wanted to add him to the collection, and there is a delight

that comes from capturing a face that is not especially strongly

featured. Currently his is my favourite picture, along with Bertrand

Russell, which has been my favourite for years.

On other occasions I might have little knowledge of the person's

work but find them interesting and enjoyable enough as characters

to want to paint. Madonna, for example, has a lovely face for

painting, and strong features, which allow for the caricature not

to lose track of what it is seeking to show (as we discussed earlier

with reference to doll-faced beauties). There is also an undeniable subversive delight in taking such an iconic and intimidating creature and exaggerating her more wildly than I do in most of my portraits, perhaps because of her extraordinary status and, as part of that, the control she must wield over images of her which are made available. I was very flattered to have one of my paintings of her featured in a book of portraits of the singer.

I might choose a subject because that individual has repeatedly popped up on the horizon of consciousness, and has therefore pushed himself forward as a suitable candidate for a portrait. The actor James Marsden, at the time of writing (though clearly not for long) slightly below the radar that signifies 'household name'

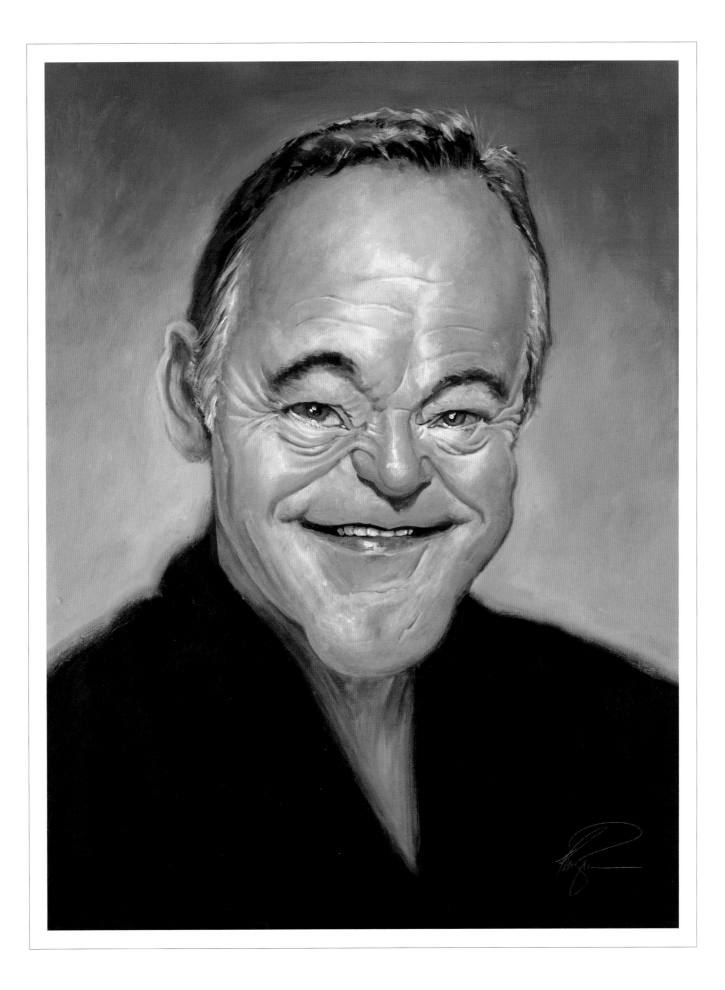

to us in the UK, appeared in a number of movies I watched in close succession: *Superman Returns*, *Enchanted*, *Hairspray* and a lovely film called *Heights* (which also features Rufus Wainwright). As a result of the appeal of Marsden's great, fifties-ish, James Dean-ish looks and a delight in his work which I suddenly kept finding without looking, he became an interesting and unobvious person to paint. Two paintings resulted – I prefer the black and white one, although his capacious grin necessitated a second portrait.

Another member of the cast of *Heights*, John Light (who introduced me to Wainwright's music, incidentally), is a good friend. I watched the movie to see his performance and that of Glenn Close, another clearly very intelligent and absorbing actor. The

opposite **TOM WAITS**

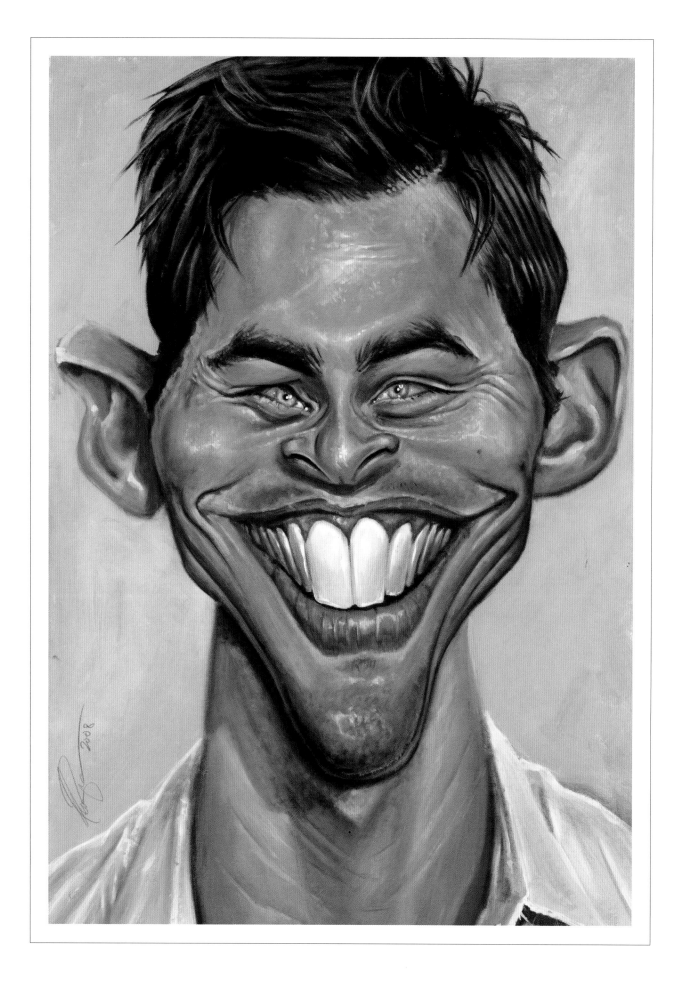

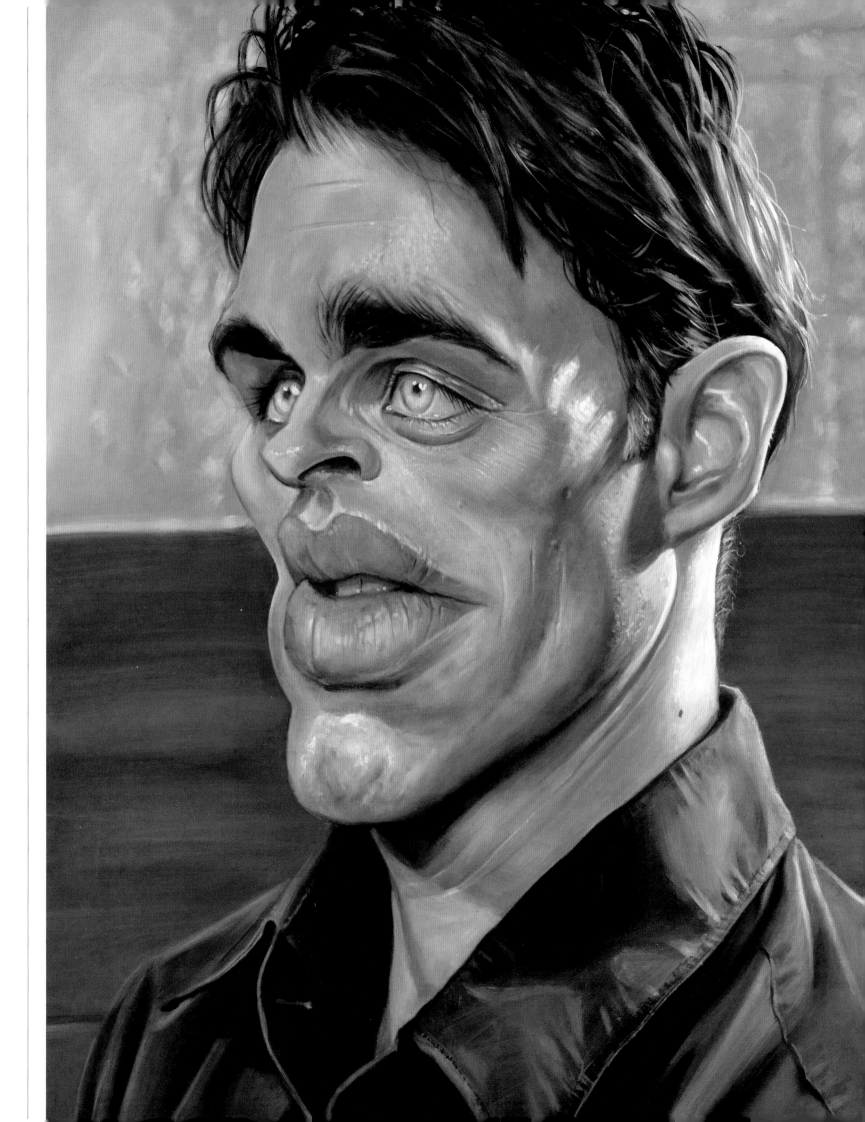

performances are astonishingly excellent throughout, so from my

enjoyment of that one film alone came three pictures: Close,

Wainwright and Marsden.

Glenn Close has a magnificent face for painting, hence her

picture inevitably emerges a little more cruelly than many of the

others. To me, it's a little reminiscent of her final scene in *Dangerous

Liaisons*, where we really get a sense of her face as a mask. I had

intended to paint her as exactly that, a disembodied mask, but

changed my mind and continued to a fuller portrait. Still, there

is something in the way her hair seems to sit *just behind* her face

that makes her skull push forward and gives her an oddly

threatening, larger-than-life physical presence on screen or stage

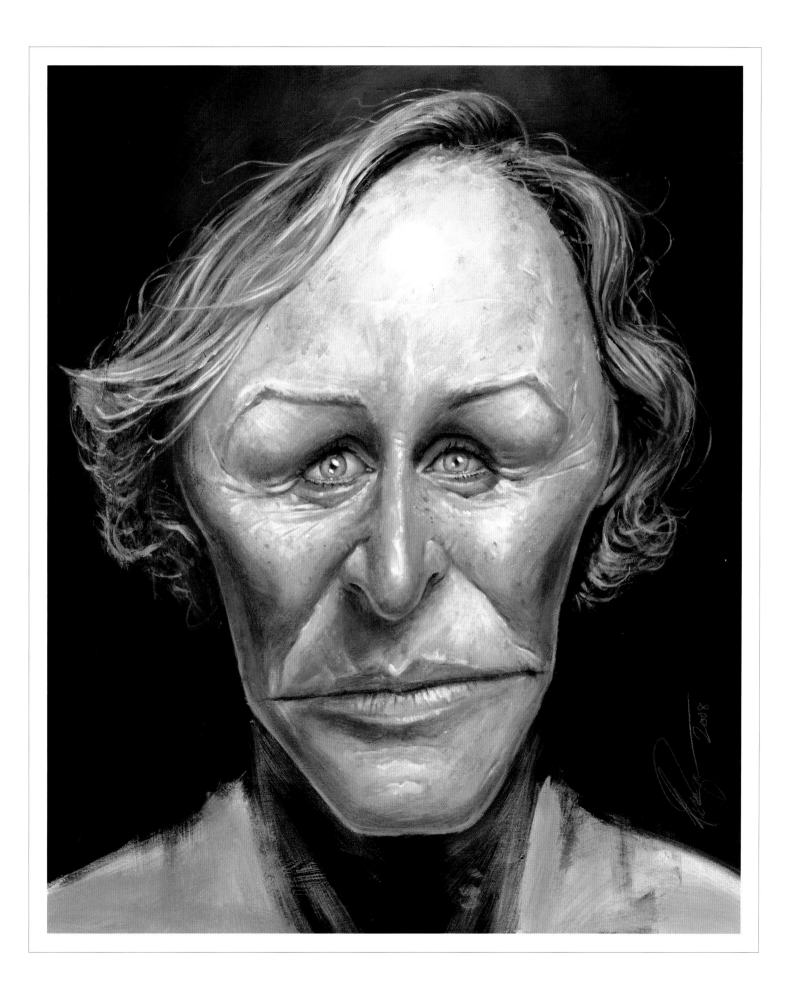

that complements her extraordinary performances and has her

devour every scene she's in. I'd wanted to paint her since

watching *Fatal Attraction*, the first 18-rated film I ever saw. I really

like the picture I have here, which was painted in a day.

This issue of cruelty in caricature is an interesting one. I am not

as interested in exaggeration for its own sake as I used to be, and am

always wary of the caricaturist's claim that it should all be seen as

a flattering tribute. Irrespective of whether the artist is being malicious

(very rare) or affectionate, if a picture is taken to be offensive, then

it simply *is* offensive, rather like the way a joke is only funny if people

laugh. I have always felt affection for my subjects as I paint them,

even more so now as I spend longer and longer working on each of them. But where there is exaggeration, there must be a reciprocal ability in the subject to laugh at himself or herself if the painting is to be well received, and the caricaturist should not privately chide the subject if such a capacity for self-mockery is not forthcoming. For this reason I have hardly ever been present on occasions when I have given a painting to subjects as a gift, for I feel they have every right not to like it and should not have to pretend that they do. I would love them to see the affection in the work – to appreciate the sheer amount of time and thought that must have gone into it, if nothing else – but I try not to expect it.

Rarely do I consciously choose how much to exaggerate. As I have mentioned, familiarity with a face makes it easier to be bold.

There is also the question of whether I want the picture to be funny. Caricaturing has its feet in trying to produce cheap laughs through exaggeration: big noses and enormous ears are unavoidably funny. A nicer, warmer humour comes from just enough exaggeration to make the viewer smile. The picture of Judi Dench always seems to prompt such a warm smile. Perhaps because there is something rather regal and untouchable about her: caused I'm sure more by shyness and professionalism than due to any grand affected style.

Rather like Stephen Fry, also featured here, Judi Dench has become a national treasure through no fault of her own. This horrendously twee epithet always seems to land on the heads of people bursting with intelligence, perspicacity and modesty, and

'I have boundless admiration for Derren's pitiless eye and have grown quite fond of his caricature.'

Stephen Fry

must rarely settle comfortably. But it does seem that in having fun with treasures such as Dench, Fry and even Her Royal Highness Herself, there is a particular, gentle pleasure to be had akin to that of teasing people we're fond of. This is quite different, for example, from our usual reaction to the exaggerated likenesses of politicians with which we are all familiar: rarely do we smile warmly when we see such pictures.

After settling on a subject, finding photographic source material is the first challenge. (At the time of writing, Stephen Fry is unique among these pages in being the only live sitter I have had the pleasure to work with in the studio, and even this was a brief sitting, long enough only to snap a few images which, due

to inebriation on my part, were in the main a little fuzzy.) Reference

photographs come from a variety of sources. I have a long shelf

of heavy books containing photographic portraits, and I will

endeavour to familiarize myself as much with my subject as these

books, my memory, DVDs and the internet will allow. I rarely do

any preliminary sketches first, unless I am truly unfamiliar with

a face. Even when I do, the original sketches have little bearing

on the finished portrait. The more familiarity there is with the face,

or the more times I have drawn or painted it in the past, the more

likely I am to want to try more dramatic exaggeration. Therefore

the more grotesque the caricatures seem, the fonder (perversely,

I suppose) I often am of the faces.

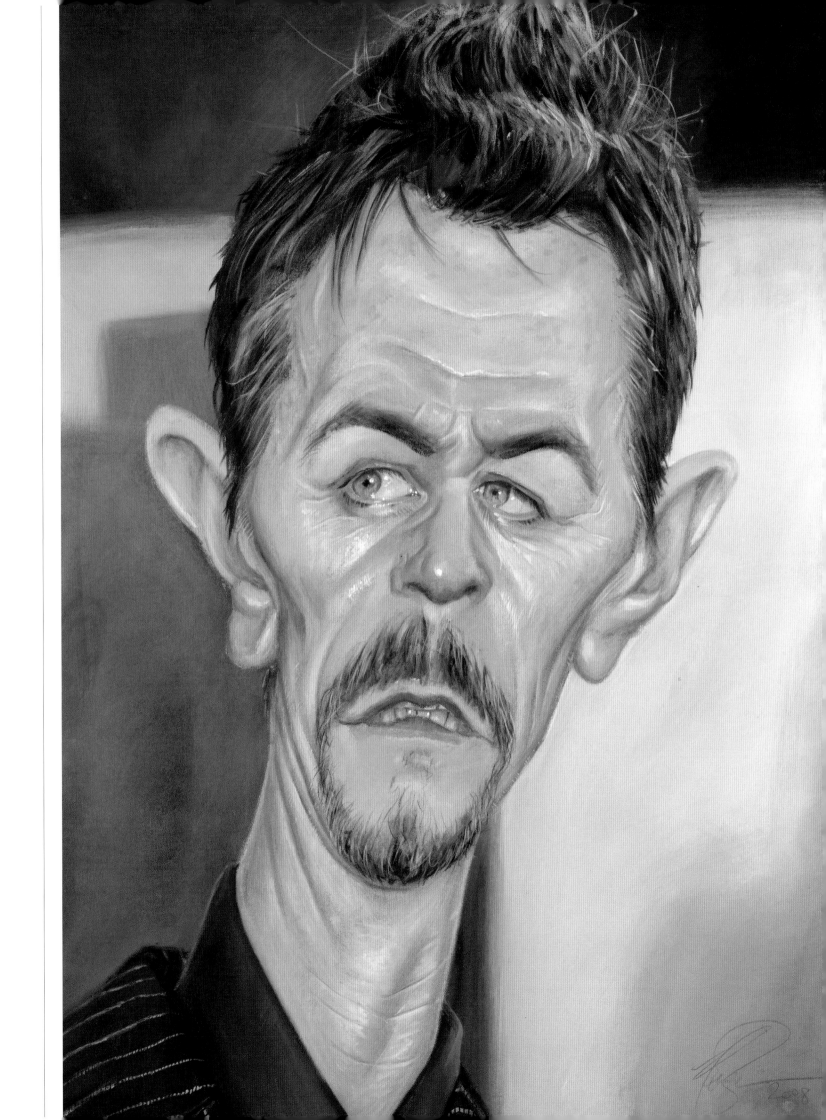

Dear Mr Brown,

I don't know you, but it seems like you know
me well. My mother saw your painting and
was amazed by the way you captured my lazy
eye (I don't know what she's talking about).
I think you brought out the mascot version
of me; that inner 'nahual' (a Mesoamerican
belief of an animal counterpart) that goes out
and plays tricks, sometimes for good and
sometimes for bad. Perhaps that's the way
I look (and feel) after a few drinks. But all
I can say in complete soberness, including
my coyote counterpart, is that it is an honour
to be one of your subjects in a painting.
Thanks for your artistry in drawing clavicles.

Gael Garcia Bernal

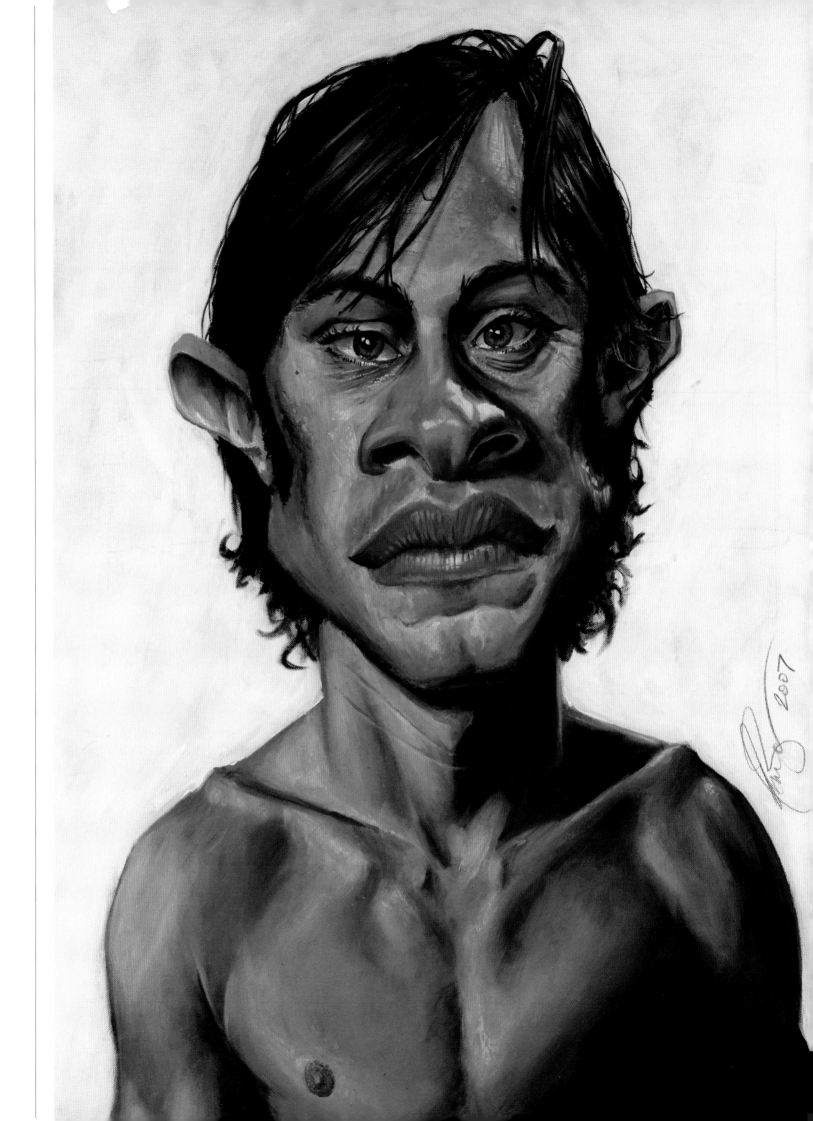

I have a small studio in my apartment devoted to the twin

tasks of painting and storing junk. The room is dominated by a

plan chest covered in tubs of acrylic, and a huge A-frame easel

which I bought from a charity shop in Bristol for five pounds.

My early pictures were painted on card, but now I work on canvas.

For a while I tried my hand at some digital paintings – a process

still carried out by hand but using the computer's palette of colours

and virtual brushes. But I can't for the life of me see the advantage,

although I wanted to after shelling out on a fancy new graphics

tablet. I have seen some impressive portraits created in this way,

where the smoothness of the finished result looks somehow too

sparkly and clean to be quite real, but the more usual result when

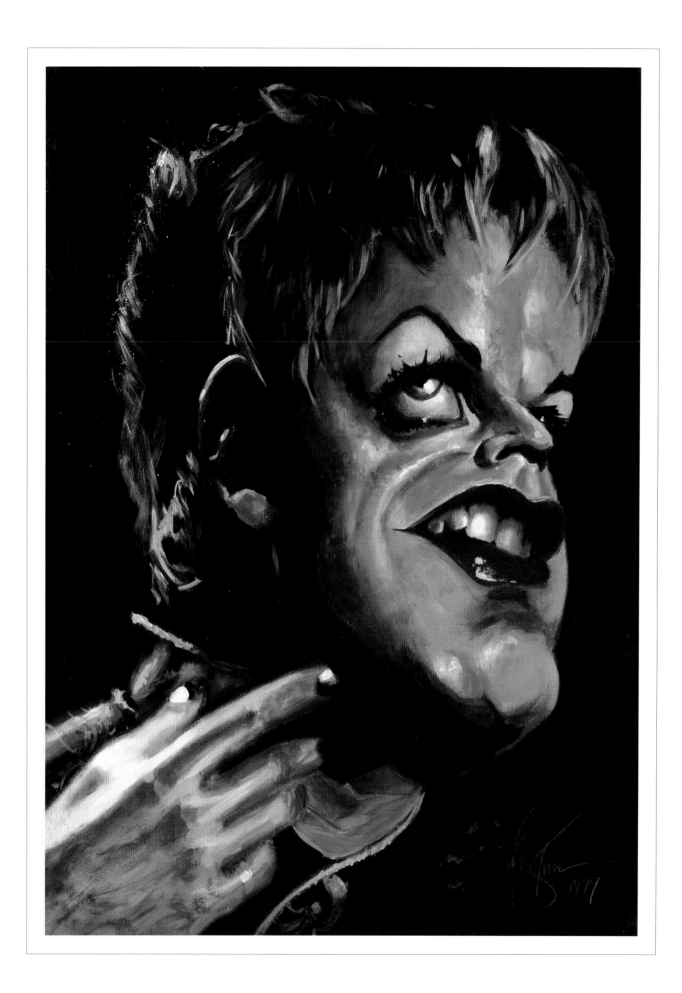

painting and blending on the computer is a slightly watery blandness that lacks the physical integrity of an oil or acrylic painting. Above all, I realized through trying these digital portraits that much of the reason for painting for me is the enjoyment of the activity itself. Standing in my studio listening to Rufus Wainwright or late-night Radio 4, holding a palette and trying paint combinations on a canvas are joys that cannot be matched by sitting in front of my computer with a tablet on my lap trying to approximate something second-best to painting. Some lovely works by digital artists reassure me that such things have their place, but for me, the process is pretty pointless.

The pictures are fairly large: the most recent canvases are four

feet high. As I've said, occasionally I sketch on a pad first; more often I draw directly with a pencil on to the canvas, and let the portrait take shape. Usually this drawing will not resemble the final product, as I know I will constantly correct and shift the picture when I apply and work the paint. If the pencil drawing is not good, I paint over the whole thing with a gesso primer or white emulsion. Then I redraw the picture while this white paint is still wet. This allows me to 'erase' lines by smearing the paint over mistakes with my finger – a much cleaner process than using an eraser which on a canvas makes a horrible mess. I use a solid graphite pencil for all of this, an HB, to avoid those dirty smudges where possible.

opposite **KIRK DOUGLAS**

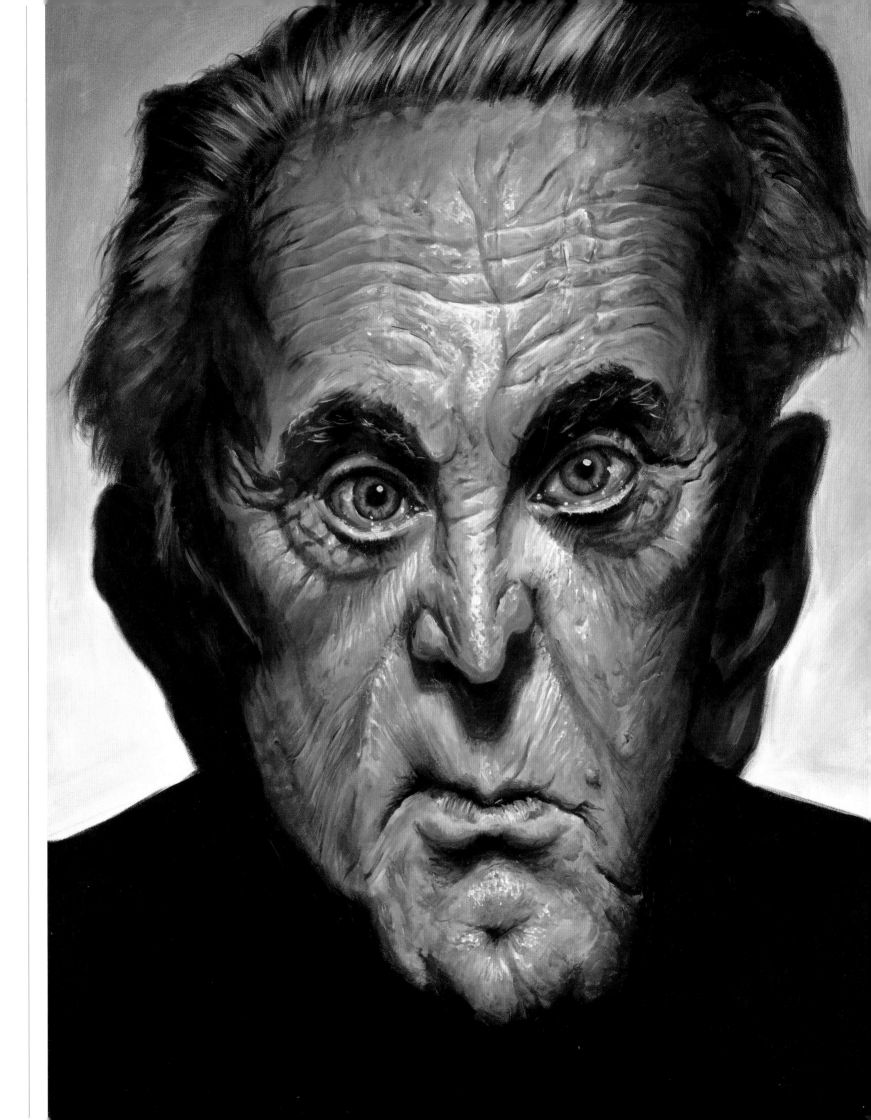

Once the drawing is done, and the composition set, I lay down some colours on the canvas, which will form the undercoat to the painting. I choose colours that I would like to peep and glow through that part of the painting: a blue beneath a white shirt, an orange beneath the skin. This use of an undercoat is a tip from Kruger's process, and I am indebted to the gifted caricaturist Neil Davies for passing it on. I have had no formal training in painting: I gave up Art A Level because I was sick of drawing peppers. For years I painted with cheap school paints I had stolen when I left that place; only through the encouragement of an artist friend was I brave enough to start with acrylics. A well-meaning but fussy friend at school had put me off them years before by telling me that I had to use acrylic colours in such-and-such an order, which sounded far too intimidating and prescriptive to bother with. Of course there are no rules with such things; exploration and enjoyment combine to form the only key. I am only now starting to experiment with gels and media to mix with the paint. I remain a very naive technician.

Painting begins generally once the undercoat is dry, and the basic areas of colour and light and shade are placed on the canvas. Beyond this, the painting develops organically in terms of how much to leave unfinished, how detailed to make it, what its relationship with its background should be. A point is usually reached that is doubtless familiar to most painters, one where the painting looks

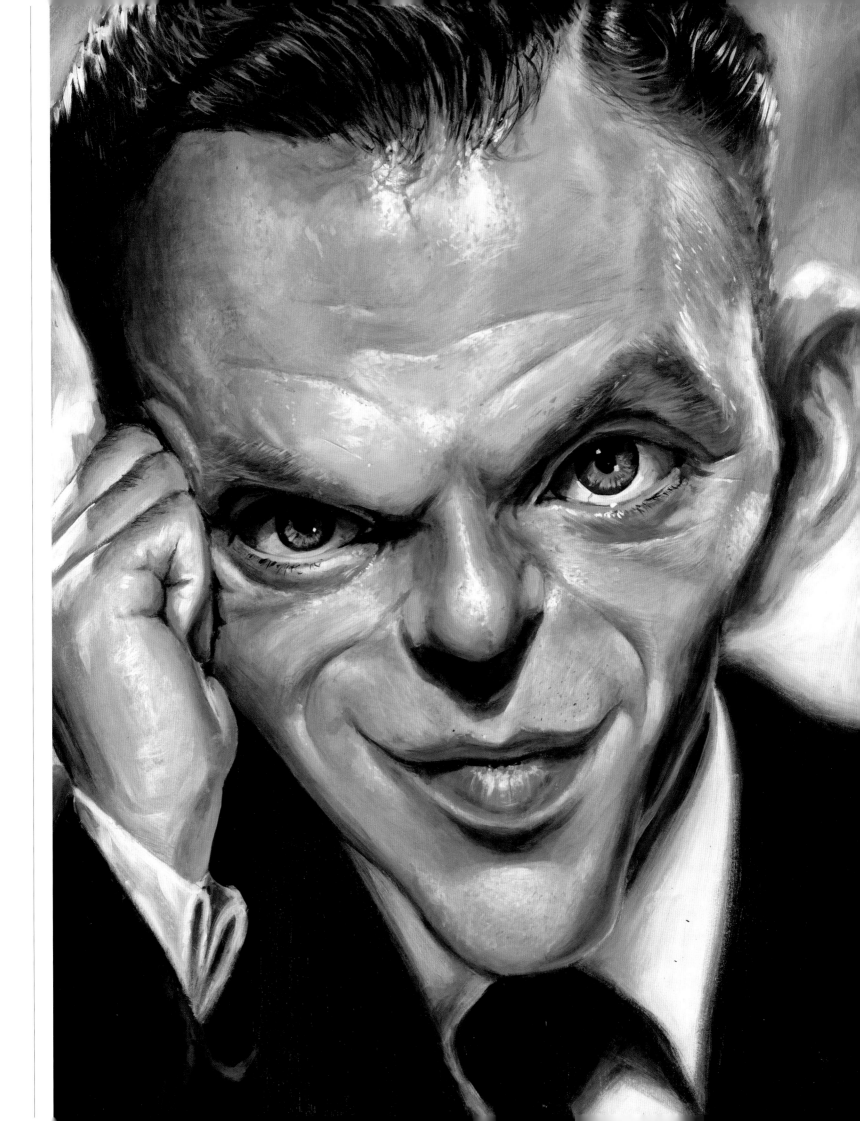

clumsy and childish. One despairs, thinking the desired result

will never be achieved. When I paint in black and white I am

haunted by the monochrome paintings of Hollywood icons I saw

as a child on the wall of the Purley Wimpy. My memory of

them (perhaps unfairly) is of washed-out, *bad* art,

not dissimilar to the inexplicable portraits of Monroe, Bogart,

Schwarzenegger and Kylie found on the sides of fairground rides.

I always reach a point when I wonder whether I have painted a

picture that would look at home on the wall of the Purley Wimpy

or the side of a waltzer. Then I must leave the painting and go

to bed: pulling oneself away and approaching one's work later

with fresh eyes is enormously important. Of course this means

opposite **ROMAN POLANSKI**

that I go to bed depressed and irritated by a work that must remain in suspended awfulness until the next morning; but a second day's work is normally enough to turn it into a decent-looking state.

For me, a curious phenomenon occurs as the painting takes shape: I hear the voice of the subject quite clearly in my head. I imagine this is not uncommon among portrait painters (I should ask around). If I do not hear the voice, the chances are the likeness has not been suitably captured. Alongside this aural effect, I also frequently catch myself adopting the same expression as the painting as I work on it, usually just *before* that twist of features is rendered in the paint: a desire to capture a certain 'look', such as Madonna's sultry, heavy, 'you know you want to' eyelids, requires,

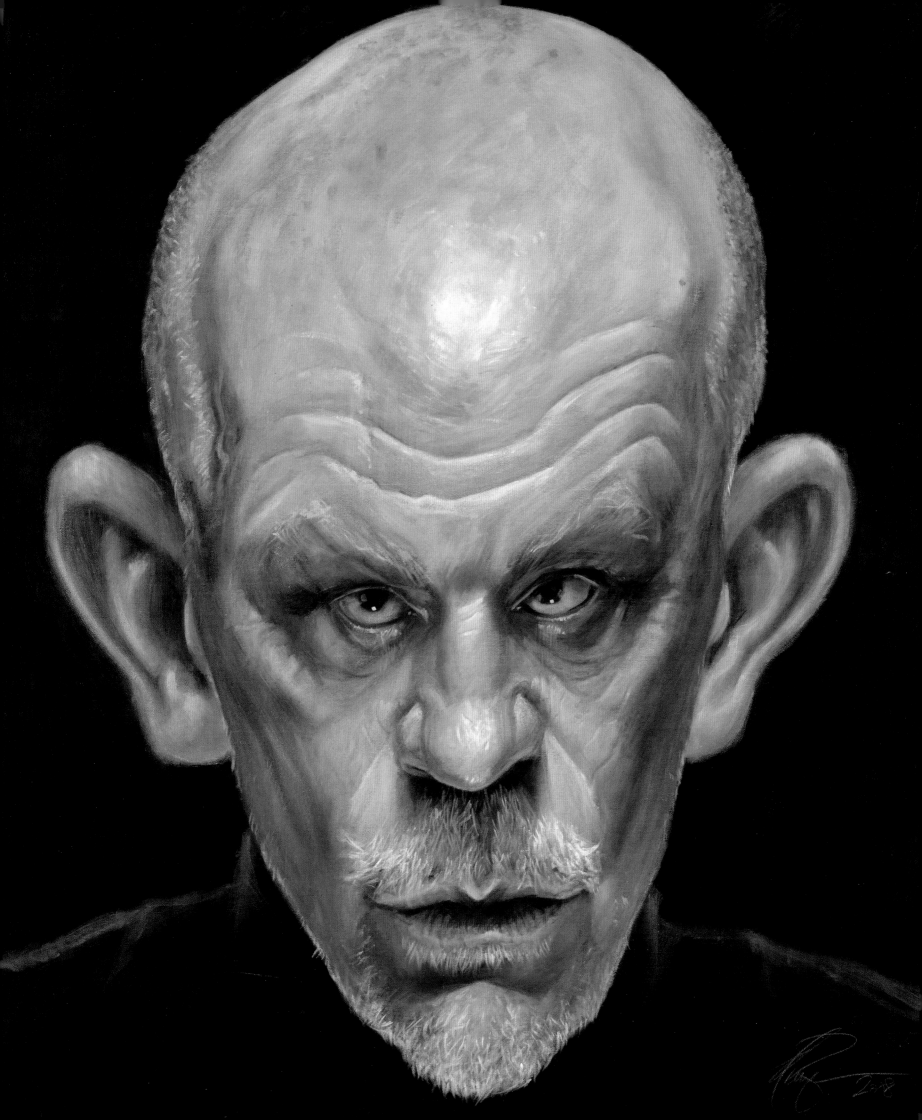

I suppose, the same emotion to run through me as I try to bring it out on the canvas. This produces a strange rapport with the emerging subject, heightened by any exaggeration in the expression being painted (and therefore the intensity of the sympathetic emotion experienced by the painter), and in turn creates a powerful, affectionate bond with the subject which is so difficult to explain in cases where a person is upset that I've made them look ugly.

When I have spent several long days or nights absorbed in every contour of a person's face and have become so familiar with their every idiosyncrasy – the asymmetry of Marsden's ears, the crack above Hopkins' left eyebrow, the bump in Brando's forehead, the

opposite **JOHNNY DEPP**

dimples and pocks in any number of faces – I just cannot help

feeling something of a one-sided special fondness for them. This

is the thin end of the obsessive wedge of course, and it is hard for

me when meeting previous subjects in real life not to feel an odd,

guilty excitement in their presence as I obsessively scan their faces

to see how those details and points of interest I spent so much time

enjoying hold up in real, three-dimensional life. If this sounds to

you like the stuff of madness, imagine the odd sensations that would

go through you if you were formally introduced to somebody who

had routinely featured in your epic masturbatory fantasies as an

adolescent. The experience is not unrelated.

Staying with that topic, at one point I thought it would be

'Well I'm just terribly honoured to be included. I think the eyebrow is a particular triumph. I had a review once saying I had the most expressive eyebrow since Roger Moore. Obviously I'd rather have had the most rugged chest since Sean Connery or the most shapely biceps since Daniel Craig, but I'll settle for the eyebrow and I think Derren has nailed it. I'm also really fucked off that Derren Brown, one of the most infuriatingly talented people I've ever met, is also an incredibly gifted painter. Unfair and, frankly, selfish.'

David Tennant

opposite **DAVID TENNANT**

'I first met Derren after the stage show in which he seemed to have memorized the entire London telephone directory – all names, numbers and addresses. Backstage he told me about this caricature but couldn't find it on his BlackBerry, and he'd forgotten where it was! Well, now it's here – and I'm delighted.'

Ian McKellen

interesting to paint the subjects naked – at least to just below the shoulders. Not obscenely or even embarrassingly, just because it seemed like an interesting idea to suggest nudity. It might feel to the viewer as if they had sat for me undressed, it would elegantly remove peripheral 'clues' to the subject's identity other than the simple facial likeness (think, for example, of an unconvincing caricature of David Beckham which might dump a football under his arm just to clarify who we are supposed to be recognizing), and most importantly, the picture would be more interesting to look at.

I soon ran into trouble with this idea, though. I was set to paint the actor Gael Garcia Bernal, and the fact that he is frequently shirtless in his films made the bare-upper-torso idea sit comfortably

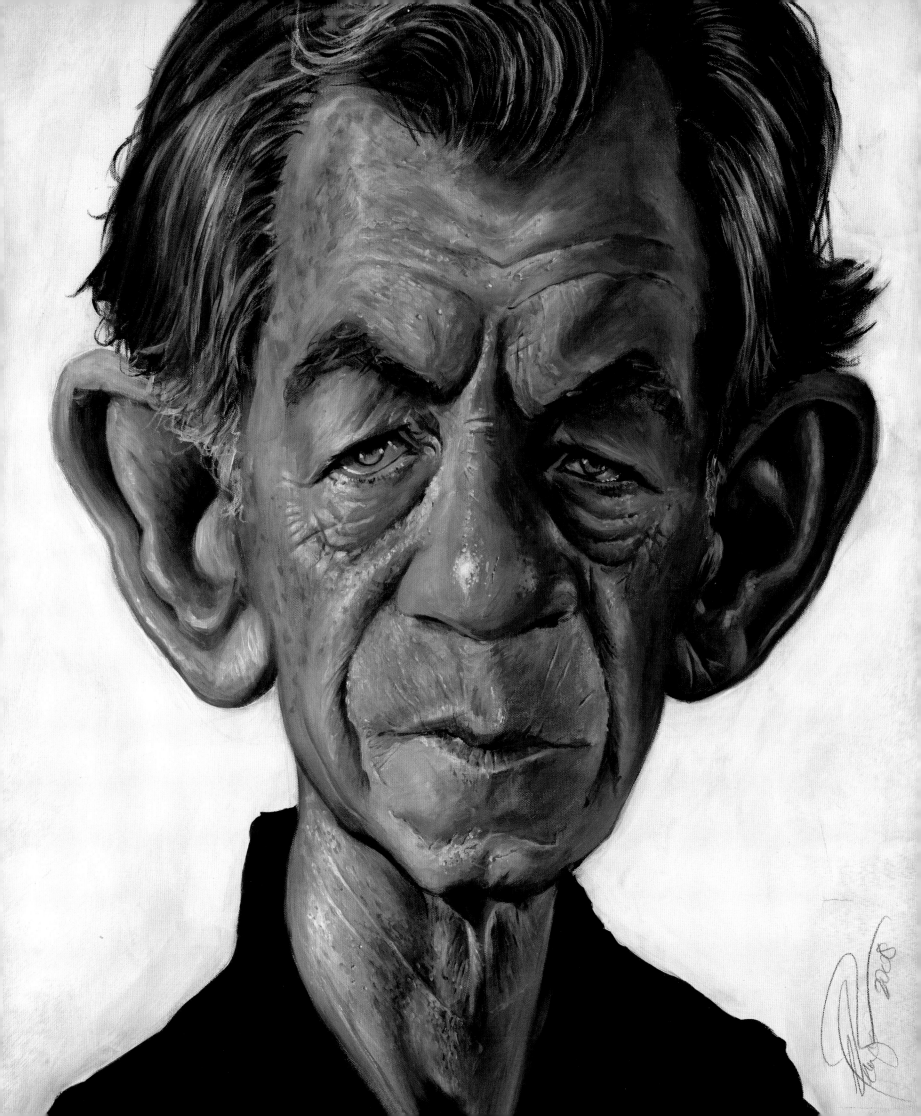

SANDRINGHAM HOUSE

19th December, 2008

Dear

    I write to thank you for the letter you have written to The Queen, with which you have enclosed a sketch for Her Majesty to see.

    I am to thank you for your kind thought.

Yours sincerely,

Susan Hussey.

Lady-in-Waiting

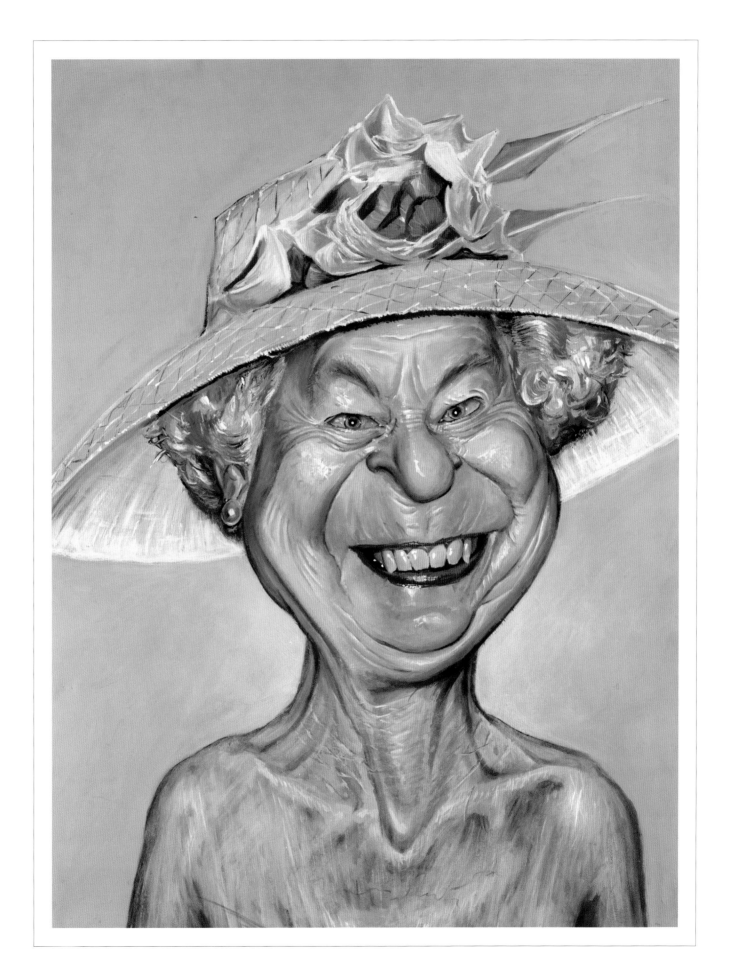

above **QUEEN ELIZABETH II**

Derren Brown

with him. Imagining a series of men and women shown like this,

I turned to another subject I had wished to paint for a while: the

Queen. Clearly the irreverent possibilities here would make for

a fun picture; I thought a hat and a grin would balance the shock

of the septuagenarian shoulders and make it seem like she was really

enjoying herself. So far so good. But next I wanted to paint Penelope

Cruz, after impossibly bumping into her at a party and deciding

that such a memorable event demanded a painting. In this case

the suggestion of nudity through bare shoulders felt redundant,

and to continue down the torso would have been to paint a very different sort of picture. I realized that we are so used to seeing images of beautiful actors, male or female, with flesh exposed that to paint them thus would not carry the impact I desired. There are, however, ways of circumnavigating this problem – unaffected expressions, blank backgrounds and simple front lighting can enhance the feel of 'nakedness' rather than 'sexiness', as well as the use of unlikely subjects – so I might return to the idea at some point. In the meantime, the current nudie series has come to a premature end.

Enjoy the pictures.

Index of Portraits